CORIOLANUS

WILLIAM SHAKESPEARE

The edition in this volume is excerpted from the multivolume "Works of William Shakespeare" collection, known as the "Cambridge Editions," edited by William George Clark (1821-1878) and William Aldis Wright (1831-1914) and published by Macmillan & Co. in 1865, which is in the public domain. No copyright claim is made with respect to public domain work.

This edition may reflect minor editorial revisions to the original text.

Cover design created using Canva.com and reproduced pursuant to its free media license agreement. Cover image is "The Constancy of Coriolanus," c. 1778, by Jean François Janinet (1752-1814), after Jean Guillaume Moitte (1746–1810) courtesy of the Metropolitan Museum of Art, Open Access/Public Domain.

CONTENTS

DRAMATIS PERSONÆ

CAIUS MARCIUS, AFTERWARDS CAIUS MARCIUS
    CORIOLANUS.
TITUS LARTIUS,
COMINIUS,
MENENIUS AGRIPPA, friend to Coriolanus.
SICINIUS VELUTUS,
JUNIUS BRUTUS,
YOUNG MARCIUS, son to Coriolanus.
A Roman Herald.
TULLUS AUFIDIUS, general of the Volscians.
Lieutenant to Aufidius.
Conspirators with Aufidius.
A Citizen of Antium.
Two Volscian Guards.
VOLUMNIA, mother to Coriolanus.
VIRGILIA, wife to Coriolanus.
VALERIA, friend to Virgilia.
Gentlewoman attending on Virgilia.
Roman and Volscian Senators, Patricians, Ædiles, Lictors,
    Soldiers, Citizens, Messengers, Servants to Aufidius,
    and other Attendants.

SCENE: Rome and the neighbourhood; Corioli and the neighbourhood; Antium

ACT I

SCENE I. ROME. A STREET

(Enter a company of mutinous Citizens, with staves, clubs, and other weapons.)

FIRST CIT. Before we proceed any further, hear me speak.
ALL. Speak, speak.
FIRST CIT. You are all resolved rather to die than to famish?
ALL. Resolved, resolved. 5
FIRST CIT. First, you know Caius Marcius is chief enemy to the people.
ALL. We know't, we know't.
FIRST CIT. Let us kill him, and we'll have corn at our own price. Is't a verdict? 10
ALL. No more talking on't; let it be done: away, away!
SEC. CIT. One word, good citizens.
FIRST CIT. We are accounted poor citizens; the patricians, good. What authority surfeits on would relieve us: if they 15 would yield us but the superfluity while it were wholesome, we might guess they relieved us humanely; but they think

we are too dear: the leanness that afflicts us, the object of
our misery, is as an inventory to particularize their
    abundance;
our sufferance is a gain to them. Let us revenge this 20
with our pikes, ere we become rakes: for the gods know I
speak this in hunger for bread, not in thirst for revenge.
SEC. CIT. Would you proceed especially against Caius
Marcius?
ALL. Against him first: he's a very dog to the 25
commonalty.
SEC. CIT. Consider you what services he has done for
his country?
FIRST CIT. Very well; and could be content to give him
good report for't, but that he pays himself with being
    proud. 30
SEC. CIT. Nay, but speak not maliciously.
FIRST CIT. I say unto you, what he hath done famously,
he did it to that end: though soft-conscienced men can be
content to say it was for his country, he did it to please his
mother and to be partly proud; which he is, even to the 35
altitude of his virtue.
SEC. CIT. What he cannot help in his nature, you account
a vice in him. You must in no way say he is covetous.
FIRST CIT. If I must not, I need not be barren of accu-
    sations;
he hath faults, with surplus, to tire in repetition. 40
(*Shouts within.*) What shouts are these? The other side o'
the city is risen: why stay we prating here? to the Capitol!
ALL. Come, come.
FIRST CIT. Soft! who comes here?
(*ENTER* MENENIUS AGRIPPA.)
SEC. CIT. Worthy Menenius Agrippa; one that hath
    always 45
loved the people.
FIRST CIT. He's one honest enough: would all the rest
were so!
MEN. What work's, my countrymen, in hand? where
    go you

With bats and clubs? the matter? speak, I pray you. 50
FIRST CIT. Our business is not unknown to the senate;
they have had inkling, this fortnight, what we intend to do,
which now we'll show 'em in deeds. They say poor suitors
have strong breaths: they shall know we have strong arms
too. 55
MEN. Why, masters, my good friends, mine honest
     neighbours,
Will you undo yourselves?
FIRST CIT. We cannot, sir, we are undone already.
MEN. I tell you, friends, most charitable care
Have the patricians of you. For your wants, 60
Your suffering in this dearth, you may as well
Strike at the heaven with your staves as lift them
Against the Roman state; whose course will on
The way it takes, cracking ten thousand curbs
Of more strong link asunder than can ever 65
Appear in your impediment. For the dearth,
The gods, not the patricians, make it, and
Your knees to them, not arms, must help. Alack,
You are transported by calamity
Thither where more attends you, and you slander 70
The helms o' the state, who care for you like fathers,
When you curse them as enemies.
FIRST CIT. Care for us! True, indeed! They ne'er
cared for us yet: suffer us to famish, and their store-houses
crammed with grain; make edicts for usury, to support 75
usurers; repeal daily any wholesome act established against
the rich, and provide more piercing statutes daily, to chain
up and restrain the poor. If the wars eat us not up, they
will; and there's all the love they bear us.
MEN. Either you must 80
Confess yourselves wondrous malicious,
Or be accused of folly. I shall tell you
A pretty tale: it may be you have heard it;
But, since it serves my purpose, I will venture
To stale't a little more. 85
FIRST CIT. Well, I'll hear it, sir: yet you must not

think to fob off our disgrace with a tale: but, an't please
you, deliver.

MEN. There was a time when all the body's members
Rebell'd against the belly; thus accused it: 90
That only like a gulf it did remain
I' the midst o' the body, idle and unactive,
Still cupboarding the viand, never bearing
Like labour with the rest; where the other instruments
Did see and hear, devise, instruct, walk, feel, 95
And, mutually participate, did minister
Unto the appetite and affection common
Of the whole body. The belly answer'd—

FIRST CIT. Well, sir, what answer made the belly?

MEN. Sir, I shall tell you. With a kind of smile, 100
Which ne'er came from the lungs, but even thus—
For, look you, I may make the belly smile
As well as speak—it tauntingly replied
To the discontented members, the mutinous parts
That envied his receipt; even so most fitly 105
As you malign our senators for that
They are not such as you.

FIRST CIT. Your belly's answer? What!
The kingly-crowned head, the vigilant eye,
The counsellor heart, the arm our soldier,
Our steed the leg, the tongue our trumpeter, 110
With other muniments and petty helps
In this our fabric, if that they—

MEN. What then?
'Fore me, this fellow speaks! what then? what then?

FIRST CIT. Should by the cormorant belly be restrain'd,
Who is the sink o' the body,—

MEN. Well, what then? 115

FIRST CIT. The former agents, if they did complain,
What could the belly answer?

MEN. I will tell you;
If you'll bestow a small—of what you have little—
Patience awhile, you'll hear the belly's answer.

FIRST CIT. You're long about it.

MEN. Note me this, good friend: 120
Your most grave belly was deliberate,
Not rash like his accusers, and thus answer'd:
'True is it, my incorporate friends,' quoth he,
'That I receive the general food at first,
Which you do live upon; and fit it is, 125
Because I am the store-house and the shop
Of the whole body: but, if you do remember,
I send it through the rivers of your blood,
Even to the court, the heart, to the seat o' the brain;
And, through the cranks and offices of man, 130
The strongest nerves and small inferior veins
From me receive that natural competency
Whereby they live: and though that all at once,
You, my good friends,'—this says the belly, mark me,—
FIRST CIT. Ay, sir; well, well.
MEN. 'Though all at once cannot 135
See what I do deliver out to each,
Yet I can make my audit up, that all
From me do back receive the flour of all,
And leave me but the bran.' What say you to't?
FIRST CIT. It was an answer: how apply you this? 140
MEN. The senators of Rome are this good belly,
And you the mutinous members: for examine
Their counsels and their cares, digest things rightly
Touching the weal o' the common, you shall find
No public benefit which you receive 145
But it proceeds or comes from them to you
And no way from yourselves. What do you think,
You, the great toe of this assembly?
FIRST CIT. I the great toe! why the great toe?
MEN. For that, being one o' the lowest, basest, poorest, 150
Of this most wise rebellion, thou go'st foremost:
Thou rascal, that art worst in blood to run,
Lead'st first to win some vantage.
But make you ready your stiff bats and clubs:
Rome and her rats are at the point of battle; 155
The one side must have bale.

(ENTER CAIUS MARCIUS.)
Hail, noble Marcius!
MAR. Thanks. What's the matter, you dissentious rogues,
That, rubbing the poor itch of your opinion,
Make yourselves scabs?
FIRST CIT. We have ever your good word.
MAR. He that will give good words to thee will flatter 160
Beneath abhorring. What would you have, you curs,
That like nor peace nor war? the one affrights you,
The other makes you proud. He that trusts to you,
Where he should find you lions, finds you hares,
Where foxes, geese: you are no surer, no, 165
Than is the coal of fire upon the ice,
Or hailstone in the sun. Your virtue is
To make him worthy whose offence subdues him
And curse that justice did it. Who deserves greatness
Deserves your hate; and your affections are 170
A sick man's appetite, who desires most that
Which would increase his evil. He that depends
Upon your favours swims with fins of lead
And hews down oaks with rushes. Hang ye! Trust ye?
With every minute you do change a mind, 175
And call him noble that was now your hate,
Him vile that was your garland. What's the matter,
That in these several places of the city
You cry against the noble senate, who,
Under the gods, keep you in awe, which else 180
Would feed on one another? What's their seeking?
MEN. For corn at their own rates; whereof, they say.
The city is well stored.
MAR. Hang 'em! They say!
They'll sit by the fire, and presume to know
What's done i' the Capitol; who's like to rise, 185
Who thrives and who declines; side factions and give out
Conjectural marriages; making parties strong,
And feebling such as stand not in their liking
Below their cobbled shoes. They say there's grain enough!
Would the nobility lay aside their ruth, 190

And let me use my sword, I'ld make a quarry
With thousands of these quarter'd slaves, as high
As I could pick my lance.
MEN. Nay, these are almost thoroughly persuaded;
For though abundantly they lack discretion, 195
Yet are they passing cowardly. But, I beseech you,
What says the other troop?
MAR. They are dissolved: hang 'em!
They said they were an-hungry; sigh'd forth proverbs,
That hunger broke stone walls, that dogs must eat,
That meat was made for mouths, that the gods sent not 200
Corn for the rich men only: with these shreds
They vented their complainings; which being answer'd,
And a petition granted them, a strange one—
To break the heart of generosity
And make bold power look pale—they threw their
        caps 205
As they would hang them on the horns o' the moon,
Shouting their emulation.
MEN. What is granted them?
MAR. Five tribunes to defend their vulgar wisdoms,
Of their own choice: one's Junius Brutus,
Sicinius Velutus, and I know not—'Sdeath! 210
The rabble should have first unroof'd the city,
Ere so prevail'd with me: it will in time
Win upon power and throw forth greater themes
For insurrection's arguing.
MEN. This is strange.
MAR. Go, get you home, you fragments! 215
(Enter a Messenger, hastily.)
MESS. Where's Caius Marcius?
MAR. Here: what's the matter?
MESS. The news is, sir, the Volsces are in arms.
MAR. I am glad on't: then we shall ha' means to vent
Our musty superfluity. See, our best elders.
*(ENTER COMINIUS, TITUS LARTIUS, AND OTHER SENATORS;
    JUNIUS BRUTUS AND SICINIUS VELUTUS.)*

FIRST SEN. Marcius, 'tis true that you have lately told
   us; 220
The Volsces are in arms.
MAR. They have a leader,
Tullus Aufidius, that will put you to't.
I sin in envying his nobility;
And were I any thing but what I am,
I would wish me only he.
COM. You have fought together. 225
MAR. Were half to half the world by the ears, and he
Upon my party, I'ld revolt, to make
Only my wars with him: he is a lion
That I am proud to hunt.
FIRST SEN. Then, worthy Marcius,
Attend upon Cominius to these wars. 230
COM. It is your former promise.
MAR. Sir, it is;
And I am constant. Titus Lartius, thou
Shalt see me once more strike at Tullus' face.
What, art thou stiff? stand'st out?
TIT. No, Caius Marcius;
I'll lean upon one crutch, and fight with t'other, 235
Ere stay behind this business.
MEN. O, true-bred!
FIRST SEN. Your company to the Capitol; where, I know,
Our greatest friends attend us.
TIT. *(To Com.)* Lead you on.
(To Mar.) Follow Cominius; we must follow you;
Right worthy you priority.
COM. Noble Marcius! 240
FIRST SEN. *(To the Citizens)* Hence to your homes; be gone!
MAR. Nay, let them follow:
The Volsces have much corn; take these rats thither
To gnaw their garners. Worshipful mutiners,
Your valour puts well forth: pray, follow.
(Citizens steal away. Exeunt all but Sicinius and Brutus.)
SIC. Was ever man so proud as is this Marcius? 245

Bru. He has no equal.

Sic. When we were chosen tribunes for the people,—

Bru. Mark'd you his lip and eyes?

Sic. Nay, but his taunts.

Bru. Being moved, he will not spare to gird the gods.

Sic. Bemock the modest moon. $_{250}$

Bru. The present wars devour him: he is grown
Too proud to be so valiant.

Sic. Such a nature,
Tickled with good success, disdains the shadow
Which he treads on at noon: but I do wonder
His insolence can brook to be commanded $_{255}$
Under Cominius.

Bru. Fame, at the which he aims,
In whom already he's well graced, can not
Better be held, nor more attain'd, than by
A place below the first: for what miscarries
Shall be the general's fault, though he perform $_{260}$
To the utmost of a man; and giddy censure
Will then cry out of Marcius 'O, if he
Had borne the business!'

Sic. Besides, if things go well,
Opinion, that so sticks on Marcius, shall
Of his demerits rob Cominius.

Bru. Come: $_{265}$
Half all Cominius' honours are to Marcius,
Though Marcius earn'd them not; and all his faults
To Marcius shall be honours, though indeed
In aught he merit not.

Sic. Let's hence, and hear
How the dispatch is made; and in what fashion, $_{270}$
More than his singularity, he goes
Upon this present action.

Bru. Let's along. (*Exeunt.*)

SCENE II. CORIOLI. THE SENATE-HOUSE

(Enter TULLUS AUFIDIUS, with Senators of Corioli.)

FIRST SEN. So, your opinion is, Aufidius,
That they of Rome are enter'd in our counsels,
And know how we proceed.
AUF. Is it not yours?
What ever have been thought on in this state,
That could be brought to bodily act ere Rome 5
Had circumvention? 'Tis not four days gone
Since I heard thence: these are the words: I think
I have the letter here: yes, here it is:
(Reads) 'They have press'd a power, but it is not known
Whether for east or west: the dearth is great; 10
The people mutinous: and it is rumour'd,
Cominius, Marcius your old enemy,
Who is of Rome worse hated than of you,
And Titus Lartius, a most valiant Roman,
These three lead on this preparation 15
Whither 'tis bent: most likely 'tis for you:
Consider of it.'
FIRST SEN. Our army's in the field:
We never yet made doubt but Rome was ready
To answer us.
AUF. Nor did you think it folly
To keep your great pretences veil'd till when 20
They needs must show themselves; which in the hatching,
It seem'd, appear'd to Rome. By the discovery
We shall be shorten'd in our aim, which was
To take in many towns ere almost Rome
Should know we were afoot.
SEC. SEN. Noble Aufidius, 25
Take your commission; hie you to your bands:
Let us alone to guard Corioli:
If they set down before 's, for the remove
Bring up your army; but, I think, you'll find
They've not prepared for us.
AUF. O, doubt not that; 30
I speak from certainties. Nay, more,

Some parcels of their power are forth already,
And only hitherward. I leave your honours.
If we and Caius Marcius chance to meet,
'Tis sworn between us, we shall ever strike ₃₅
Till one can do no more.
ALL. The gods assist you!
AUF. And keep your honours safe!
FIRST SEN. *Farewell.*
SEC. SEN. Farewell.
ALL. Farewell. (*Exeunt.*)

SCENE III. ROME. A ROOM IN MARCIUS' HOUSE.

(Enter VOLUMNIA and VIRGILIA: they set them down on two low stools, and sew.)

VOL. I pray you, daughter, sing, or express yourself in a
more comfortable sort: if my son were my husband, I
    should
freelier rejoice in that absence wherein he won honour than
in the embracements of his bed where he would show most
love. When yet he was but tender-bodied, and the only
    son ₅
of my womb; when youth with comeliness plucked all gaze
his way; when, for a day of kings' entreaties, a mother
should not sell him an hour from her beholding; I,
    considering
how honour would become such a person; that it
was no better than picture-like to hang by the wall, if
    renown ₁₀
made it not stir, was pleased to let him seek danger where
he was like to find fame. To a cruel war I sent him; from
whence he returned, his brows bound with oak. I tell thee,
daughter, I sprang not more in joy at first hearing he was
a man-child than now in first seeing he had proved
    himself ₁₅
a man.

VIR. But had he died in the business, madam: how then?

VOL. Then his good report should have been my son; I therein would have found issue. Hear me profess sincerely: had I a dozen sons, each in my love alike, and none less dear than thine and my good Marcius, I had rather had eleven die nobly for their country than one voluptuously surfeit out of action.

(Enter a Gentlewoman.*)*

GENT. Madam, the Lady Valeria is come to visit you.

VIR. Beseech you, give me leave to retire myself.

VOL. Indeed, you shall not.
Methinks I hear hither your husband's drum;
See him pluck Aufidius down by the hair;
As children from a bear, the Volsces shunning him:
Methinks I see him stamp thus, and call thus:
'Come on, you cowards! you were got in fear,
Though you were born in Rome:' his bloody brow
With his mail'd hand then wiping, forth he goes,
Like to a harvest-man that's task'd to mow
Or all, or lose his hire.

VIR. His bloody brow! O Jupiter, no blood!

VOL. Away, you fool! it more becomes a man
Than gilt his trophy: the breasts of Hecuba,
When she did suckle Hector, look'd not lovelier
Than Hector's forehead when it spit forth blood
At Grecian sword, contemning. Tell Valeria
We are fit to bid her welcome. *(Exit Gent.)*

VIR. Heavens bless my lord from fell Aufidius!

VOL. He'll beat Aufidius' head below his knee,
And tread upon his neck.

(Enter VALERIA, *with an* Usher *and* Gentlewoman.*)*

VAL. My ladies both, good day to you.

VOL. Sweet madam.

VIR. I am glad to see your ladyship.

VAL. How do you both? you are manifest house-keepers.
What are you sewing here? A fine spot, in good faith.
How does your little son?

VIR. I thank your ladyship; well, good madam.

VOL. He had rather see the swords and hear a drum
than look upon his schoolmaster.

VAL. O' my word, the father's son: I'll swear, 'tis a very 55
pretty boy. O' my troth, I looked upon him o' Wednesday
half an hour together: has such a confirmed countenance.
I saw him run after a gilded butterfly; and when he caught
it, he let it go again; and after it again; and over and over
he comes, and up again; catched it again: or whether his 60
fall enraged him, or how 'twas, he did so set his teeth, and
tear it; O, I warrant, how he mammocked it!

VOL. One on 's father's moods.

VAL. Indeed, la, 'tis a noble child.

VIR. A crack, madam. 65

VAL. Come, lay aside your stitchery; I must have you
play the idle huswife with me this afternoon.

VIR. No, good madam; I will not out of doors.

VAL. Not out of doors!

VOL. She shall, she shall. 70

VIR. Indeed, no, by your patience; I'll not over the
threshold till my lord return from the wars.

VAL. Fie, you confine yourself most unreasonably:
come, you must go visit the good lady that lies in.

VIR. I will wish her speedy strength, and visit her with 75
my prayers; but I cannot go thither.

VOL. Why, I pray you?

VIR. 'Tis not to save labour, nor that I want love.

VAL. You would be another Penelope: yet, they say, all
the yarn she spun in Ulysses' absence did but fill Ithaca 80
full of moths. Come; I would your cambric were sensible
as your finger, that you might leave pricking it for pity.
Come, you shall go with us.

VIR. No, good madam, pardon me; indeed, I will not
forth. 85

VAL. In truth, la, go with me, and I'll tell you excellent
news of your husband.

VIR. O, good madam, there can be none yet.

VAL. Verily, I do not jest with you; there came news
from him last night. ₉₀

VIR. Indeed, madam?

VAL. In earnest, it's true; I heard a senator speak it.
Thus it is: the Volsces have an army forth; against whom
Cominius the general is gone, with one part of our Roman
power: your lord and Titus Lartius are set down before ₉₅
their city Corioli; they nothing doubt prevailing, and to
make it brief wars. This is true, on mine honour; and so,
I pray, go with us.

VIR. Give me excuse, good madam; I will obey you
in every thing hereafter. ₁₀₀

VOL. Let her alone, lady; as she is now, she will but
disease our better mirth.

VAL. In troth, I think she would. Fare you well,
then. Come, good sweet lady. Prithee, Virgilia, turn thy
solemness out o' door, and go along with us. ₁₀₅

VIR. No, at a word, madam; indeed, I must not. I
wish you much mirth.

VAL. Well then, farewell. (*Exeunt.*)

SCENE IV. BEFORE CORIOLI

*(Enter, with drum and colours, MARCIUS, TITUS LARTIUS, Captains and
Soldiers. To them a Messenger.)*

MAR. Yonder comes news: a wager they have met.

LART. My horse to yours, no.

MAR. 'Tis done.

LART. Agreed.

MAR. Say, has our general met the enemy?

MESS. They lie in view; but have not spoke as yet.

LART. So, the good horse is mine.

MAR. I'll buy him of you. ₅

LART. No, I'll nor sell nor give him: lend you him I will
For half a hundred years. Summon the town.

MAR. How far off lie these armies?

MESS. Within this mile and half.

MAR. Then shall we hear their 'larum, and they ours.

Now, Mars, I prithee, make us quick in work, 10

That we with smoking swords may march from hence,

To help our fielded friends! Come, blow thy blast.

(They sound a parley. Enter two Senators with others, on the walls.)

Tullus Aufidius, is he within your walls?

FIRST SEN. No, nor a man that fears you less than he,

That's lesser than a little. Hark, our drums 15

(Drum afar off.)

Are bringing forth our youth! we'll break our walls,

Rather than they shall pound us up: our gates,

Which yet seem shut, we have but pinn'd with rushes;

They'll open of themselves. Hark you, far off!

(Alarum far off.)

There is Aufidius; list, what work he makes 20

Amongst your cloven army.

MAR. O, they are at it!

LART. Their noise be our instruction. Ladders, ho!

(Enter the army of the Volsces.)

MAR. They fear us not, but issue forth their city.

Now put your shields before your hearts, and fight

With hearts more proof than shields. Advance, brave

Titus: 25

They do disdain us much beyond our thoughts,

Which makes me sweat with wrath. Come on, my fellows:

He that retires, I'll take him for a Volsce,

And he shall feel mine edge.

(Alarum. The Romans are beat back to their trenches. Re-enter

MARCIUS, cursing.)

MAR. All the contagion of the south light on you, 30

You shames of Rome! you herd of—Boils and plagues

Plaster you o'er; that you may be abhorr'd

Farther than seen, and one infect another

Against the wind a mile! You souls of geese,

That bear the shapes of men, how have you run 35

From slaves that apes would beat! Pluto and hell!

All hurt behind; backs red, and faces pale

With flight and agued fear! Mend, and charge home,
Or, by the fires of heaven, I'll leave the foe,
And make my wars on you: look to 't: come on; ₄₀
If you'll stand fast, we'll beat them to their wives,
As they us to our trenches followed.
(Another alarum. The Volsces fly, and MARCIUS follows them to the
gates.)
So, now the gates are ope: now prove good seconds:
'Tis for the followers fortune widens them,
Not for the fliers: mark me, and do the like. ₄₅
(Enters the gates.)
FIRST SOL. Fool-hardiness; not I.
SEC. SOL. *Nor I. (Marcius is shut in.)*
FIRST SOL. See, they have shut him in.
ALL. To the pot, I warrant him.
(Alarum continues.)
(RE-ENTER TITUS LARTIUS.)
LART. What is become of Marcius?
ALL. Slain, sir, doubtless.
FIRST SOL. Following the fliers at the very heels, ₅₀
With them he enters; who, upon the sudden,
Clapp'd to their gates: he is himself alone,
To answer all the city.
LART. O noble fellow!
Who sensibly outdares his senseless sword,
And, when it bows, stands up! Thou art left, Marcius: ₅₅
A carbuncle entire, as big as thou art,
Were not so rich a jewel. Thou wast a soldier
Even to Cato's wish, not fierce and terrible
Only in strokes; but, with thy grim looks and
The thunder-like percussion of thy sounds, ₆₀
Thou madest thine enemies shake, as if the world
Were feverous and did tremble.
(Re-enter MARCIUS, bleeding, assaulted by the enemy.)
FIRST SOL. Look, sir.
LART. O, 'tis Marcius!
Let's fetch him off, or make remain alike.
(They fight, and all enter the city.)

SCENE V. WITHIN CORIOLI. A STREET

(Enter certain Romans, with spoils.)

FIRST ROM. This will I carry to Rome.
SEC. ROM. And I this.
THIRD ROM. A murrain on't! I took this for silver.
(Alarum continues still afar off.)
(Enter MARCIUS and TITUS LARTIUS with a trumpet.)
MAR. See here these movers that do prize their hours
At a crack'd drachma! Cushions, leaden spoons, 5
Irons of a doit, doublets that hangmen would
Bury with those that wore them, these base slaves,
Ere yet the fight be done, pack up: down with them!
And hark, what noise the general makes! To him!
There is the man of my soul's hate, Aufidius, 10
Piercing our Romans: then, valiant Titus, take
Convenient numbers to make good the city;
Whilst I, with those that have the spirit, will haste
To help Cominius.
LART. Worthy sir, thou bleed'st;
Thy exercise hath been too violent 15
For a second course of fight.
MAR. Sir, praise me not;
My work hath yet not warm'd me: fare you well:
The blood I drop is rather physical
Than dangerous to me: to Aufidius thus
I will appear, and fight.
LART. Now the fair goddess, Fortune, 20
Fall deep in love with thee; and her great charms
Misguide thy opposers' swords! Bold gentleman,
Prosperity be thy page!
MAR. Thy friend no less
Than those she placeth highest! So farewell.
LART. Thou worthiest Marcius! *(Exit Marcius.)* 25
Go, sound thy trumpet in the market-place;
Call thither all the officers o' the town,

Where they shall know our mind. Away! (*Exeunt.*)

SCENE VI. NEAR THE CAMP OF COMINIUS

(*Enter COMINIUS, as it were in retire, with Soldiers.*)

COM. Breathe you, my friends: well fought; we are
    come off
Like Romans, neither foolish in our stands
Nor cowardly in retire: believe me, sirs,
We shall be charged again. Whiles we have struck,
By interims and conveying gusts we have heard 5
The charges of our friends. Ye Roman gods,
Lead their successes as we wish our own,
That both our powers, with smiling fronts encountering,
May give you thankful sacrifice!
(*Enter a* Messenger.)
Thy news?
MESS. The citizens of Corioli have issued, 10
And given to Lartius and to Marcius battle:
I saw our party to their trenches driven,
And then I came away.
COM. Though thou speak'st truth,
Methinks thou speak'st not well. How long is't since?
MESS. Above an hour, my lord. 15
COM. 'Tis not a mile; briefly we heard their drums:
How couldst thou in a mile confound an hour,
And bring thy news so late?
MESS. Spies of the Volsces
Held me in chase, that I was forced to wheel
Three or four miles about; else had I, sir, 20
Half an hour since brought my report.
(*ENTER* MARCIUS.)
COM. Who's yonder,
That does appear as he were flay'd? O gods!
He has the stamp of Marcius; and I have
Before-time seen him thus.

MAR. Come I too late?

COM. The shepherd knows not thunder from a tabor 25
More than I know the sound of Marcius' tongue
From every meaner man.

MAR. Come I too late?

COM. Ay, if you come not in the blood of others,
But mantled in your own.

MAR. O, let me clip ye
In arms as sound as when I woo'd; in heart 30
As merry as when our nuptial day was done,
And tapers burn'd to bedward!

COM. Flower of warriors,
How is't with Titus Lartius?

MAR. As with a man busied about decrees:
Condemning some to death, and some to exile; 35
Ransoming him or pitying, threatening the other;
Holding Corioli in the name of Rome,
Even like a fawning greyhound in the leash,
To let him slip at will.

COM. Where is that slave
Which told me they had beat you to your trenches? 40
Where is he? call him hither.

MAR. Let him alone;
He did inform the truth: but for our gentlemen,
The common file—a plague! tribunes for them!—
The mouse ne'er shunn'd the cat as they did budge
From rascals worse than they.

COM. But how prevail'd you? 45

MAR. Will the time serve to tell? I do not think.
Where is the enemy? are you lords o' the field?
If not, why cease you till you are so?

COM. Marcius,
We have at disadvantage fought and did
Retire to win our purpose. 50

MAR. How lies their battle? know you on which side
They have placed their men of trust?

COM. As I guess, Marcius,

Their bands i' the vaward are the Antiates,
Of their best trust; o'er them Aufidius,
Their very heart of hope.

MAR. I do beseech you, 55
By all the battles wherein we have fought,
By the blood we have shed together, by the vows
We have made to endure friends, that you directly
Set me against Aufidius and his Antiates;
And that you not delay the present, but, 60
Filling the air with swords advanced and darts,
We prove this very hour.

COM. Though I could wish
You were conducted to a gentle bath,
And balms applied to you, yet dare I never
Deny your asking: take your choice of those 65
That best can aid your action.

MAR. Those are they
That most are willing. If any such be here—
As it were sin to doubt—that love this painting
Wherein you see me smear'd; if any fear
Lesser his person than an ill report; 70
If any think brave death outweighs bad life,
And that his country's dearer than himself;
Let him alone, or so many so minded,
Wave thus, to express his disposition,
And follow Marcius. 75

*(They all shout, and wave their swords; take him up in their arms,
    and cast up their caps.)*

O, me alone! make you a sword of me?
If these shows be not outward, which of you
But is four Volsces? none of you but is
Able to bear against the great Aufidius
A shield as hard as his. A certain number, 80
Though thanks to all, must I select from all: the rest
Shall bear the business in some other fight,
As cause will be obey'd. Please you to march;
And four shall quickly draw out my command,
Which men are best inclined.

COM. March on, my fellows: 85
Make good this ostentation, and you shall
Divide in all with us. (*Exeunt.*)

SCENE VII. THE GATES OF CORIOLI

(*TITUS LARTIUS, having set a guard upon Corioli, going with drum and trumpet toward COMINIUS and CAIUS MARCIUS, enters with a Lieutenant, other Soldiers, and a Scout.*)

LART. So, let the ports be guarded: keep your duties,
As I have set them down. If I do send, dispatch
Those centuries to our aid; the rest will serve
For a short holding: if we lose the field,
We cannot keep the town.
LIEU. Fear not our care, sir. 5
LART. Hence, and shut your gates upon 's.
Our guider, come; to the Roman camp conduct us. (*Exeunt.*)

SCENE VIII. A FIELD OF BATTLE BETWEEN THE ROMAN AND THE VOLSCIAN CAMPS.

(*Alarum as in battle. Enter, from opposite sides, MARCIUS and AUFIDIUS.*)

MAR. I'll fight with none but thee; for I do hate thee
Worse than a promise-breaker.
AUF. We hate alike:
Not Afric owns a serpent I abhor
More than thy fame and envy. Fix thy foot.
MAR. Let the first budger die the other's slave, 5
And the gods doom him after!
AUF. If I fly, Marcius,
Holloa me like a hare.
MAR. Within these three hours, Tullus,
Alone I fought in your Corioli walls,
And made what work I pleased: 'tis not my blood
Wherein thou seest me mask'd; for thy revenge 10

Wrench up thy power to the highest.
AUF. Wert thou the Hector
That was the whip of your bragg'd progeny,
Thou shouldst not 'scape me here.
(They fight, and certain Volsces come in the aid of Aufidius. Marcius
fights till they be driven in breathless.)
Officious, and not valiant, you have shamed me
In your condemned seconds. (*Exeunt.*) 15

SCENE IX. THE ROMAN CAMP

Flourish. Alarum. A retreat is sounded. Enter, from one side, COMINIUS with
the Romans; from the other side, MARCIUS, with his arm in a scarf.

COM. If I should tell thee o'er this thy day's work,
Thou'ldst not believe thy deeds: but I'll report it,
Where senators shall mingle tears with smiles;
Where great patricians shall attend, and shrug,
I' the end admire; where ladies shall be frighted, 5
And, gladly quaked, hear more; where the dull tribunes,
That, with the fusty plebeians, hate thine honours,
Shall say against their hearts 'We thank the gods
Our Rome hath such a soldier.'
Yet camest thou to a morsel of this feast, 10
Having fully dined before.
(Enter TITUS LARTIUS, with his power, from the pursuit.)
LART. O general,
Here is the steed, we the caparison:
Hadst thou beheld—
MAR. Pray now, no more: my mother,
Who has a charter to extol her blood,
When she does praise me grieves me. I have done 15
As you have done; that's what I can: induced
As you have been; that's for my country:
He that has but effected his good will
Hath overta'en mine act.
COM. You shall not be

The grave of your deserving; Rome must know $_{20}$
The value of her own: 'twere a concealment
Worse than a theft, no less than a traducement,
To hide your doings; and to silence that,
Which, to the spire and top of praises vouch'd,
Would seem but modest: therefore, I beseech you— $_{25}$
In sign of what you are, not to reward
What you have done—before our army hear me.

MAR. I have some wounds upon me, and they smart
To hear themselves remember'd.

COM. Should they not,
Well might they fester 'gainst ingratitude, $_{30}$
And tent themselves with death. Of all the horses,
Whereof we have ta'en good, and good store, of all
The treasure in this field achieved and city,
We render you the tenth; to be ta'en forth,
Before the common distribution, at $_{35}$
Your only choice.

MAR. I thank you, general;
But cannot make my heart consent to take
A bribe to pay my sword: I do refuse it,
And stand upon my common part with those
That have beheld the doing. $_{40}$

*(A long flourish. They all cry 'Marcius! Marcius!' cast up their caps
      and lances: Cominius and Lartius stand bare.)*

MAR. May these same instruments, which you profane,
Never sound more! when drums and trumpets shall
I' the field prove flatterers, let courts and cities be
Made all of false-faced soothing!
When steel grows soft as the parasite's silk, $_{45}$
Let him be made a coverture for the wars!
No more, I say! For that I have not wash'd
My nose that bled, or foil'd some debile wretch,
Which without note here's many else have done,
You shout me forth $_{50}$
In acclamations hyperbolical;
As if I loved my little should be dieted
In praises sauced with lies.

Com. Too modest are you;
More cruel to your good report than grateful
To us that give you truly: by your patience, 55
If 'gainst yourself you be incensed, we'll put you,
Like one that means his proper harm, in manacles,
Then reason safely with you. Therefore, be it known,
As to us, to all the world, that Caius Marcius
Wears this war's garland: in token of the which, 60
My noble steed, known to the camp, I give him,
With all his trim belonging; and from this time,
For what he did before Corioli, call him,
With all the applause and clamour of the host,
Caius Marcius Coriolanus. Bear 65
The addition nobly ever! (Flourish. Trumpets sound, and drums.)
All. Caius Marcius Coriolanus!
Cor. I will go wash;
And when my face is fair, you shall perceive
Whether I blush, or no: howbeit, I thank you: 70
I mean to stride your steed; and at all times
To undercrest your good addition
To the fairness of my power.
Com. So, to our tent;
Where, ere we do repose us, we will write
To Rome of our success. You, Titus Lartius, 75
Must to Corioli back: send us to Rome
The best, with whom we may articulate
For their own good and ours.
Lart. I shall, my lord.
Cor. The gods begin to mock me. I, that now
Refused most princely gifts, am bound to beg 80
Of my lord general.
Com. Take 't; 'tis yours. What is't?
Cor. I sometime lay here in Corioli
At a poor man's house; he used me kindly:
He cried to me; I saw him prisoner;
But then Aufidius was within my view, 85
And wrath o'erwhelm'd my pity: I request you
To give my poor host freedom.

COM. O, well begg'd!
Were he the butcher of my son, he should
Be free as is the wind. Deliver him, Titus.
LART. Marcius, his name?
COR. By Jupiter, forgot: 90
I am weary; yea, my memory is tired.
Have we no wine here?
COM. Go we to our tent:
The blood upon your visage dries; 'tis time
It should be look'd to: come. (*Exeunt.*)

SCENE X. THE CAMP OF THE VOLSCES

(A flourish. Cornets. Enter TULLUS AUFIDIUS, bloody, with two or three Soldiers.)

AUF. The town is ta'en!
FIRST SOL. 'Twill be deliver'd back on good condition.
AUF. Condition!
I would I were a Roman; for I cannot,
Being a Volsce, be that I am. Condition! 5
What good condition can a treaty find
I' the part that is at mercy? Five times, Marcius,
I have fought with thee; so often hast thou beat me;
And wouldst do so, I think, should we encounter
As often as we eat. By the elements, 10
If e'er again I meet him beard to beard,
He's mine, or I am his: mine emulation
Hath not that honour in 't it had; for where
I thought to crush him in an equal force,
True sword to sword, I'll potch at him some way, 15
Or wrath or craft may get him.
FIRST SOL. He's the devil.
AUF. Bolder, though not so subtle. My valour's poison'd
With only suffering stain by him; for him
Shall fly out of itself: nor sleep nor sanctuary,
Being naked, sick, nor fane nor Capitol, 20

The prayers of priests nor times of sacrifice,
Embarquements all of fury, shall lift up
Their rotten privilege and custom 'gainst
My hate to Marcius: where I find him, were it
At home, upon my brother's guard, even there, 25
Against the hospitable canon, would I
Wash my fierce hand in's heart. Go you to the city;
Learn how 'tis held, and what they are that must
Be hostages for Rome.

FIRST SOL. Will not you go?

AUF. I am attended at the cypress grove: I pray you— 30
'Tis south the city mills—bring me word thither
How the world goes, that to the pace of it
I may spur on my journey.

FIRST SOL. *I shall, sir. (Exeunt.)*

ACT II

SCENE I. ROME. A PUBLIC PLACE

(Enter MENENIUS, with the two Tribunes of the people, SICINIUS, and BRUTUS.)

MEN. The augurer tells me we shall have news to-night.
BRU. Good or bad?
MEN. Not according to the prayer of the people, for
they love not Marcius.
SIC. Nature teaches beasts to know their friends. ₅
MEN. Pray you, who does the wolf love?
SIC. The lamb.
MEN. Ay, to devour him; as the hungry plebeians would
the noble Marcius.
BRU. He's a lamb indeed, that baes like a bear. ₁₀
MEN. He's a bear indeed, that lives like a lamb. You
two are old men: tell me one thing that I shall ask you.
BOTH. Well, sir.
MEN. In what enormity is Marcius poor in, that you
two have not in abundance? ₁₅
BRU. He's poor in no one fault, but stored with all.
SIC. Especially in pride.

BRU. And topping all others in boasting.

MEN. This is strange now: do you two know how you
are censured here in the city, I mean of us o' the
    right-hand 20
file? do you?

BOTH. Why, how are we censured?

MEN. Because you talk of pride now,—will you not be
angry?

BOTH. Well, well, sir, well. 25

MEN. Why, 'tis no great matter; for a very little thief of
occasion will rob you of a great deal of patience: give your
dispositions the reins, and be angry at your pleasures; at
the least, if you take it as a pleasure to you in being so.
You blame Marcius for being proud? 30

BRU. We do it not alone, sir.

MEN. I know you can do very little alone; for your helps
are many, or else your actions would grow wondrous single:
your abilities are too infant-like for doing much alone. You
talk of pride: O that you could turn your eyes toward the 35
napes of your necks, and make but an interior survey of
your good selves! O that you could!

BOTH. What then, sir?

MEN. Why, then you should discover a brace of
    unmeriting,
proud, violent, testy magistrates, alias fools, as 40
any in Rome.

SIC. Menenius, you are known well enough too.

MEN. I am known to be a humorous patrician, and one
that loves a cup of hot wine with not a drop of allaying
    Tiber
in't; said to be something imperfect in favouring the first 45
complaint, hasty and tinder-like upon too trivial motion;
one that converses more with the buttock of the night than
with the forehead of the morning: what I think I utter, and
spend my malice in my breath. Meeting two such wealsmen
as you are,—I cannot call you Lycurguses—if the drink 50
you give me touch my palate adversely, I make a crooked
face at it. I can't say your worships have delivered the

matter well, when I find the ass in compound with the
    major
part of your syllables: and though I must be content to bear
with those that say you are reverend grave men, yet they 55
lie deadly that tell you you have good faces. If you see this
in the map of my microcosm, follows it that I am known
well enough too? what harm can your bisson conspectuities
glean out of this character, if I be known well enough too?
BRU. Come, sir, come, we know you well enough. 60
MEN. You know neither me, yourselves, nor any thing.
You are ambitious for poor knaves' caps and legs: you wear
out a good wholesome forenoon in hearing a cause
    between
an orange-wife and a fosset-seller, and then rejourn the
    controversy
of three-pence to a second day of audience. When 65
you are hearing a matter between party and party, if you
chance to be pinched with the colic, you make faces like
mummers; set up the bloody flag against all patience; and,
in roaring for a chamber-pot, dismiss the controversy
    bleeding,
the more entangled by your hearing: all the peace you 70
make in their cause is, calling both the parties knaves. You
are a pair of strange ones.
BRU. Come, come, you are well understood to be a
    perfecter
giber for the table than a necessary bencher in the
Capitol. 75
MEN. Our very priests must become mockers, if they
shall encounter such ridiculous subjects as you are. When
you speak best unto the purpose, it is not worth the
    wagging
of your beards; and your beards deserve not so honourable
a grave as to stuff a botcher's cushion, or to be entombed 80
in an ass's pack-saddle. Yet you must be saying, Marcius is
proud; who, in a cheap estimation, is worth all your prede-
    cessors
since Deucalion; though peradventure some of the

best of 'em were hereditary hangmen. God-den to your
worships: more of your conversation would infect my
   brain, 85
being the herdsmen of the beastly plebeians: I will be bold
to take my leave of you. (Brutus and Sicinius go aside.)
(ENTER VOLUMNIA, VIRGILIA, *AND* VALERIA.*)*
How now, my as fair as noble ladies,—and the moon, were
she earthly, no nobler—whither do you follow your eyes so
fast? 90
VOL. Honourable Menenius, my boy Marcius approaches;
for the love of Juno, let's go.
MEN. Ha! Marcius coming home!
VOL. Ay, worthy Menenius; and with most prosperous
approbation. 95
MEN. Take my cap, Jupiter, and I thank thee. Hoo!
Marcius coming home!
VIR. & VAL. Nay, 'tis true.
VOL. Look, here's a letter from him: the state hath
another, his wife another; and, I think, there's one at
   home 100
for you.
MEN. I will make my very house reel to-night: a letter
for me!
VIR. Yes, certain, there's a letter for you; I saw 't.
MEN. A letter for me! it gives me an estate of seven 105
years' health; in which time I will make a lip at the
   physician:
the most sovereign prescription in Galen is but empiricutic,
and, to this preservative, of no better report than a
horse-drench. Is he not wounded? he was wont to come
home wounded. 110
VIR. O, no, no, no.
VOL. O, he is wounded; I thank the gods for't.
MEN. So do I too, if it be not too much: brings a' victory
in his pocket? the wounds become him.
VOL. On's brows: Menenius, he comes the third time 115
home with the oaken garland.
MEN. Has he disciplined Aufidius soundly?

VOL. Titus Lartius writes, they fought together, but
Aufidius got off.

MEN. And 'twas time for him too, I'll warrant him that: 120
an he had stayed by him, I would not have been so fidiused
for all the chests in Corioli, and the gold that's in them. Is
the senate possessed of this?

VOL. Good ladies, let's go. Yes, yes, yes; the senate has
letters from the general, wherein he gives my son the
whole 125
name of the war: he hath in this action outdone his former
deeds doubly.

VAL. In troth, there's wondrous things spoke of him.

MEN. Wondrous! ay, I warrant you, and not without
his true purchasing. 130

VIR. The gods grant them true!

VOL. True! pow, wow.

MEN. True! I'll be sworn they are true. Where is he
wounded? (*To the Tribunes*) God save your good worships!
Marcius is coming home: he has more cause to be 135
proud. Where is he wounded?

VOL. I' the shoulder and i' the left arm: there will be
large cicatrices to show the people, when he shall stand for
his place. He received in the repulse of Tarquin seven
hurts i' the body. 140

MEN. One i' the neck, and two i' the thigh; there's nine
that I know.

VOL. He had, before this last expedition, twenty five
wounds upon him.

MEN. Now it's twenty seven: every gash was an enemy's 145
grave. (*A shout and flourish.*) Hark! the trumpets.

VOL. These are the ushers of Marcius: before him he
carries noise, and behind him he leaves tears:
Death, that dark spirit, in's nervy arm doth lie;
Which, being advanced, declines, and then men die. 150

(*A sennet. Trumpets sound. Enter* COMINIUS *and* TITUS LARTIUS;
between them, CORIOLANUS, *crowned with an oaken garland;*
with Captains and Soldiers, and a Herald.)

HER. Know, Rome, that all alone Marcius did fight
Within Corioli gates: where he hath won,
With fame, a name to Caius Marcius; these
In honour follows Coriolanus.
Welcome to Rome, renowned Coriolanus! (*Flourish.*) 155
ALL. Welcome to Rome, renowned Coriolanus!
COR. No more of this, it does offend my heart;
Pray now, no more.
COM. Look, sir, your mother!
COR. O,
You have, I know, petition'd all the gods
For my prosperity! (*Kneels.*)
VOL. Nay, my good soldier, up; 160
My gentle Marcius, worthy Caius, and
By deed-achieving honour newly named,—
What is it?—Coriolanus must I call thee?—
But, O, thy wife!
COR. My gracious silence, hail!
Wouldst thou have laugh'd had I come coffin'd home, 165
That weep'st to see me triumph? Ah, my dear,
Such eyes the widows in Corioli wear,
And mothers that lack sons.
MEN. Now, the gods crown thee!
COR. And live you yet? (*To Valeria*) O my sweet lady,
    pardon.
VOL. I know not where to turn: O, welcome home: 170
And welcome, general: and ye're welcome all.
MEN. A hundred thousand welcomes. I could weep
And I could laugh, I am light and heavy. Welcome:
A curse begin at very root on's heart,
That is not glad to see thee! You are three 175
That Rome should dote on: yet, by the faith of men,
We have some old crab-trees here at home that will not
Be grafted to your relish. Yet welcome, warriors:
We call a nettle but a nettle, and
The faults of fools but folly.
COM. Ever right. 180
COR. Menenius, ever, ever.

HER. Give way there, and go on.
COR. *(To Volumnia and Virgilia) Your hand, and yours:*
Ere in our own house I do shade my head,
The good patricians must be visited;
From whom I have received not only greetings, 185
But with them change of honours.
VOL. I have lived
To see inherited my very wishes
And the buildings of my fancy: only
There's one thing wanting, which I doubt not but
Our Rome will cast upon thee.
COR. Know, good mother, 190
I had rather be their servant in my way
Than sway with them in theirs.
COM. On, to the Capitol!
(Flourish. Cornets. Exeunt in state, as before. Brutus and Sicinius
come forward.)
BRU. All tongues speak of him, and the bleared sights
Are spectacled to see him: your prattling nurse
Into a rapture lets her baby cry 195
While she chats him: the kitchen malkin pins
Her richest lockram 'bout her reechy neck,
Clambering the walls to eye him: stalls, bulks, windows,
Are smother'd up, leads fill'd and ridges horsed
With variable complexions, all agreeing 200
In earnestness to see him: seld-shown flamens
Do press among the popular throngs, and puff
To win a vulgar station: our veil'd dames
Commit the war of white and damask in
Their nicely-gawded cheeks to the wanton spoil 205
Of Phœbus' burning kisses: such a pother,
As if that whatsoever god who leads him
Were slily crept into his human powers,
And gave him graceful posture.
SIC. On the sudden,
I warrant him consul.
BRU. Then our office may, 210
During his power, go sleep.

S*ic*. He cannot temperately transport his honours
From where he should begin and end, but will
Lose those he hath won.

B*ru*. In that there's comfort.

S*ic*. Doubt not
The commoners, for whom we stand, but they
Upon their ancient malice will forget
With the least cause these his new honours; which
That he will give them make I as little question
As he is proud to do 't.

B*ru*. I heard him swear,
Were he to stand for consul, never would he
Appear i' the market-place, nor on him put
The napless vesture of humility,
Nor showing, as the manner is, his wounds
To the people, beg their stinking breaths.

S*ic*. 'Tis right.

B*ru*. It was his word: O, he would miss it rather
Than carry it but by the suit of the gentry to him
And the desire of the nobles.

S*ic*. I wish no better
Than have him hold that purpose and to put it
In execution.

B*ru*. 'Tis most like he will.

S*ic*. It shall be to him then, as our good wills,
A sure destruction.

B*ru*. So it must fall out
To him or our authorities. For an end,
We must suggest the people in what hatred
He still hath held them; that to's power he would
Have made them mules, silenced their pleaders and
Dispropertied their freedoms; holding them,
In human action and capacity,
Of no more soul nor fitness for the world
Than camels in the war, who have their provand
Only for bearing burthens, and sore blows
For sinking under them.

S*ic*. This, as you say, suggested

At some time when his soaring insolence
Shall touch the people—which time shall not want,
If he be put upon 't; and that's as easy
As to set dogs on sheep—will be his fire 245
To kindle their dry stubble; and their blaze
Shall darken him for ever.
(Enter a Messenger.)
BRU. What's the matter?
MESS. You are sent for to the Capitol. 'Tis thought
That Marcius shall be consul:
I have seen the dumb men throng to see him and 250
The blind to hear him speak: matrons flung gloves,
Ladies and maids their scarfs and handkerchers,
Upon him as he pass'd: the nobles bended,
As to Jove's statue, and the commons made
A shower and thunder with their caps and shouts: 255
I never saw the like.
BRU. Let's to the Capitol,
And carry with us ears and eyes for the time,
But hearts for the event.
SIC. Have with you. (*Exeunt.*)

SCENE II. THE SAME. THE CAPITOL

(Enter two Officers, to lay cushions.)

FIRST OFF. Come, come, they are almost here. How
many stand for consulships?
SEC. OFF. Three, they say: but 'tis thought of every
one Coriolanus will carry it.
FIRST OFF. That's a brave fellow; but he's vengeance 5
proud, and loves not the common people.
SEC. OFF. Faith, there have been many great men that
have flattered the people, who ne'er loved them; and there
be many that they have loved, they know not wherefore: so
that, if they love they know not why, they hate upon no 10
better a ground: therefore, for Coriolanus neither to care

whether they love or hate him manifests the true knowledge
he has in their disposition; and out of his noble carelessness
lets them plainly see 't.

FIRST OFF. If he did not care whether he had their love 15
or no, he waved indifferently 'twixt doing them neither
        good
nor harm: but he seeks their hate with greater devotion
than they can render it him, and leaves nothing undone
that may fully discover him their opposite. Now, to seem
to affect the malice and displeasure of the people is as
        bad 20
as that which he dislikes, to flatter them for their love.

SEC. OFF. He hath deserved worthily of his country: and
his ascent is not by such easy degrees as those who, having
been supple and courteous to the people, bonneted,
        without
any further deed to have them at all into their estimation 25
and report: but he hath so planted his honours in their
eyes and his actions in their hearts, that for their tongues
to be silent and not confess so much, were a kind of
        ingrateful
injury; to report otherwise were a malice that,
giving itself the lie, would pluck reproof and rebuke from 30
every ear that heard it.

FIRST OFF. No more of him; he's a worthy man: make
way, they are coming.

(A sennet. Enter, with Lictors before them, COMINIUS the Consul,
    MENENIUS, CORIOLANUS, Senators, SICINIUS and BRUTUS.
    The Senators take their places; the Tribunes take their place by
    themselves. CORIOLANUS stands.)

MEN. Having determined of the Volsces and
To send for Titus Lartius, it remains, 35
As the main point of this our after-meeting,
To gratify his noble service that
Hath thus stood for his country: therefore, please you,
Most reverend and grave elders, to desire
The present consul, and last general 40
In our well-found successes, to report

A little of that worthy work perform'd
By Caius Marcius Coriolanus; whom
We met here, both to thank and to remember
With honours like himself.

FIRST SEN. Speak, good Cominius: 45
Leave nothing out for length, and make us think
Rather our state's defective for requital
Than we to stretch it out. (*To the Tribunes*) Masters o' the
    people,
We do request your kindest ears, and after,
Your loving motion toward the common body, 50
To yield what passes here.

SIC. We are convented
Upon a pleasing treaty, and have hearts
Inclinable to honour and advance
The theme of our assembly.

BRU. Which the rather
We shall be bless'd to do, if he remember 55
A kinder value of the people than
He hath hereto prized them at.

MEN. That's off, that's off;
I would you rather had been silent. Please you
To hear Cominius speak?

BRU. Most willingly:
But yet my caution was more pertinent 60
Than the rebuke you give it.

MEN. He loves your people;
But tie him not to be their bedfellow.
Worthy Cominius, speak. (Coriolanus offers to go away.)
Nay, keep your place.

FIRST SEN. Sit, Coriolanus; never shame to hear
What you have nobly done.

COR. Your honours' pardon: 65
I had rather have my wounds to heal again
Than hear say how I got them.

BRU. Sir, I hope
My words disbench'd you not.

COR. No, sir: yet oft,

When blows have made me stay, I fled from words.
You sooth'd not, therefore hurt not: but your people, 70
I love them as they weigh.
MEN. Pray now, sit down.
COR. I had rather have one scratch my head i' the sun
When the alarum were struck than idly sit
To hear my nothings monster'd. (*Exit.*)
MEN. Masters of the people,
Your multiplying spawn how can he flatter— 75
That's thousand to one good one—when you now see
He had rather venture all his limbs for honour
Than one on's ears to hear it? Proceed, Cominius.
COM. I shall lack voice: the deeds of Coriolanus
Should not be utter'd feebly. It is held 80
That valour is the chiefest virtue and
Most dignifies the haver: if it be,
The man I speak of cannot in the world
Be singly counterpoised. At sixteen years,
When Tarquin made a head for Rome, he fought 85
Beyond the mark of others: our then dictator,
Whom with all praise I point at, saw him fight,
When with his Amazonian chin he drove
The bristled lips before him: he bestrid
An o'er-press'd Roman, and i' the consul's view 90
Slew three opposers: Tarquin's self he met,
And struck him on his knee: in that day's feats,
When he might act the woman in the scene,
He proved best man i' the field, and for his meed
Was brow-bound with the oak. His pupil age 95
Man-enter'd thus, he waxed like a sea;
And, in the brunt of seventeen battles since,
He lurch'd all swords of the garland. For this last,
Before and in Corioli, let me say,
I cannot speak him home: he stopp'd the fliers; 100
And by his rare example made the coward
Turn terror into sport: as weeds before
A vessel under sail, so men obey'd,
And fell below his stem: his sword, death's stamp,

Where it did mark, it took; from face to foot $_{105}$
He was a thing of blood, whose every motion
Was timed with dying cries: alone he enter'd
The mortal gate of the city, which he painted
With shunless destiny; aidless came off,
And with a sudden re-enforcement struck $_{110}$
Corioli like a planet: now all's his:
When, by and by, the din of war gan pierce
His ready sense; then straight his doubled spirit
Re-quicken'd what in flesh was fatigate,
And to the battle came he; where he did $_{115}$
Run reeking o'er the lives of men, as if
'Twere a perpetual spoil: and till we call'd
Both field and city ours, he never stood
To ease his breast with panting.
MEN. Worthy man!
FIRST SEN. He cannot but with measure fit the honours $_{120}$
Which we devise him.
COM. Our spoils he kick'd at,
And look'd upon things precious, as they were
The common muck of the world: he covets less
Than misery itself would give; rewards
His deeds with doing them, and is content $_{125}$
To spend the time to end it.
MEN. He's right noble:
Let him be call'd for.
FIRST SEN. Call Coriolanus.
OFF. He doth appear.
(RE-ENTER CORIOLANUS.*)*
MEN. The senate, Coriolanus, are well pleased
To make thee consul.
COR. I do owe them still $_{130}$
My life and services.
MEN. It then remains
That you do speak to the people.
COR. I do beseech you,
Let me o'erleap that custom, for I cannot
Put on the gown, stand naked, and entreat them,

For my wounds' sake, to give their suffrage: please you ₁₃₅
That I may pass this doing.
Sic. Sir, the people
Must have their voices; neither will they bate
One jot of ceremony.
Men. Put them not to't:
Pray you, go fit you to the custom, and
Take to you, as your predecessors have, ₁₄₀
Your honour with your form.
Cor. It is a part
That I shall blush in acting, and might well
Be taken from the people.
Bru. Mark you that?
Cor. To brag unto them, thus I did, and thus;
Show them the unaching scars which I should hide, ₁₄₅
As if I had received them for the hire
Of their breath only!
Men. Do not stand upon't.
We recommend to you, tribunes of the people,
Our purpose to them: and to our noble consul
Wish we all joy and honour. ₁₅₀
Senators. To Coriolanus come all joy and honour!
(Flourish of cornets. Exeunt all but Sicinius and Brutus.)
Bru. You see how he intends to use the people.
Sic. May they perceive's intent! He will require them,
As if he did contemn what he requested
Should be in them to give.
Bru. Come, we'll inform them ₁₅₅
Of our proceedings here: on the market-place,
I know, they do attend us. *(Exeunt.)*

SCENE III. THE SAME. THE FORUM

(Enter seven or eight Citizens.)

First Cit. Once, if he do require our voices, we ought
not to deny him.

SEC. CIT. We may, sir, if we will.

THIRD CIT. We have power in ourselves to do it, but it is a power that we have no power to do: for if he show us his wounds and tell us his deeds, we are to put our tongues into those wounds and speak for them; so, if he tell us his noble deeds, we must also tell him our noble acceptance of them. Ingratitude is monstrous: and for the multitude to be ingrateful, were to make a monster of the multitude; of the which we being members, should bring ourselves to be monstrous members.

FIRST CIT. And to make us no better thought of, a little help will serve; for once we stood up about the corn, he himself stuck not to call us the many-headed multitude.

THIRD CIT. We have been called so of many; not that our heads are some brown, some black, some auburn, some bald, but that our wits are so diversely coloured: and truly I think, if all our wits were to issue out of one skull, they would fly east, west, north, south, and their consent of one direct way should be at once to all the points o' the compass.

SEC. CIT. Think you so? Which way do you judge my wit would fly?

THIRD CIT. Nay, your wit will not so soon out as another man's will; 'tis strongly wedged up in a block-head; but if it were at liberty, 'twould, sure, southward.

SEC. CIT. Why that way?

THIRD CIT. To lose itself in a fog; where being three parts melted away with rotten dews, the fourth would return for conscience sake, to help to get thee a wife.

SEC. CIT. You are never without your tricks: you may, you may.

THIRD CIT. Are you all resolved to give your voices? But that's no matter, the greater part carries it. I say, if he would incline to the people, there was never a worthier man.

(Enter CORIOLANUS in a gown of humility, with MENENIUS.)
Here he comes, and in the gown of humility: mark his
    behaviour.
We are not to stay all together, but to come by him
where he stands, by ones, by twos, and by threes. He's to
make his requests by particulars; wherein every one of us
has a single honour, in giving him our own voices with
    our $_{40}$
own tongues: therefore follow me, and I'll direct you how
you shall go by him.
ALL. *Content, content. (Exeunt Citizens.)*
MEN. O sir, you are not right: have you not known
The worthiest men have done 't?
COR. What must I say?— $_{45}$
'I pray, sir,'—Plague upon 't! I cannot bring
My tongue to such a pace. 'Look, sir, my wounds!
I got them in my country's service, when
Some certain of your brethren roar'd and ran
From the noise of our own drums.'
MEN. O me, the gods! $_{50}$
You must not speak of that: you must desire them
To think upon you.
COR. Think upon me! hang 'em!
I would they would forget me, like the virtues
Which our divines lose by 'em.
MEN. You'll mar all:
I'll leave you: pray you, speak to 'em, I pray you, $_{55}$
In wholesome manner. (*Exit.*)
COR. Bid them wash their faces,
And keep their teeth clean. (*Re-enter two of the Citizens.*)
So, here comes a brace.
(Re-enter a third Citizen.)
You know the cause, sir, of my standing here.
THIRD CIT. We do, sir; tell us what hath brought you
to 't. $_{60}$
COR. Mine own desert.
SEC. CIT. Your own desert!
COR. Ay, but not mine own desire.

FIRST CIT. How! not your own desire!

COR. No, sir, 'twas never my desire yet to trouble the 65
poor with begging.

THIRD CIT. You must think, if we give you any thing,
we hope to gain by you.

COR. Well then, I pray, your price o' the consulship?

FIRST CIT. The price is, to ask it kindly. 70

COR. Kindly! Sir, I pray, let me ha 't: I have wounds
to show you, which shall be yours in private. Your good
voice, sir; what say you?

SEC. CIT. You shall ha' it, worthy sir.

COR. A match, sir. There's in all two worthy voices 75
begged. I have your alms: adieu.

THIRD CIT. But this is something odd.

SEC. CIT. An 'twere to give again,—but 'tis no matter.

(Exeunt the three Citizens.)

(Re-enter two other Citizens.)

COR. Pray you now, if it may stand with the tune of
your voices that I may be consul, I have here the customary

80
gown.

FOURTH CIT. You have deserved nobly of your country,
and you have not deserved nobly.

COR. Your enigma?

FOURTH CIT. You have been a scourge to her enemies, 85
you have been a rod to her friends; you have not indeed
loved the common people.

COR. You should account me the more virtuous, that I
have not been common in my love. I will, sir, flatter my
sworn brother, the people, to earn a dearer estimation of 90
them; 'tis a condition they account gentle: and since the
wisdom of their choice is rather to have my hat than my
heart, I will practise the insinuating nod and be off to
them most counterfeitly; that is, sir, I will counterfeit the
bewitchment of some popular man, and give it bountiful

to 95
the desirers. Therefore, beseech you, I may be consul.

FIFTH CIT. We hope to find you our friend; and therefore give you our voices heartily.

FOURTH CIT. You have received many wounds for your country. 100

COR. I will not seal your knowledge with showing them. I will make much of your voices, and so trouble you no farther.

BOTH CIT. The gods give you joy, sir, heartily! (*Exeunt.*)

COR. Most sweet voices! 105
Better it is to die, better to starve,
Than crave the hire which first we do deserve.
Why in this woolvish toge should I stand here,
To beg of Hob and Dick that do appear,
Their needless vouches? Custom calls me to 't: 110
What custom wills, in all things should we do 't,
The dust on antique time would lie unswept,
And mountainous error be too highly heap'd
For truth to o'er-peer. Rather than fool it so,
Let the high office and the honour go 115
To one that would do thus. I am half through:
The one part suffer'd, the other will I do.
(*Re-enter three Citizens more.*)
Here come moe voices.
Your voices: for your voices I have fought;
Watch'd for your voices; for your voices bear 120
Of wounds two dozen odd; battles thrice six
I have seen, and heard of; for your voices have
Done many things, some less, some more: your voices:
Indeed, I would be consul.

SIXTH CIT. He has done nobly, and cannot go without 125 any honest man's voice.

SEVENTH CIT. Therefore let him be consul: the gods give him joy, and make him good friend to the people!

ALL. Amen, amen. God save thee, noble consul!
(*Exeunt*)

COR. Worthy voices! 130

(*RE-ENTER MENENIUS, WITH BRUTUS AND SICINIUS.*)

MEN. You have stood your limitation; and the tribunes

Endue you with the people's voice: remains
That in the official marks invested in you
Anon do meet the senate.
COR. Is this done?
SIC. The custom of request you have discharged: 135
The people do admit you, and are summon'd
To meet anon upon you approbation.
COR. Where? at the senate-house?
SIC. There, Coriolanus.
COR. May I change these garments?
SIC. You may, sir.
COR. That I'll straight do, and, knowing myself again, 140
Repair to the senate-house.
MEN. I'll keep you company. Will you along?
BRU. We stay here for the people.
SIC. Fare you well.
(Exeunt Coriolanus and Menenius.)
He has it now; and, by his looks, methinks
'Tis warm at's heart.
BRU. With a proud heart he wore 145
His humble weeds. Will you dismiss the people?
(Re-enter Citizens.)
SIC. How now, my masters! have you chose this man?
FIRST CIT. He has our voices, sir.
BRU. We pray the gods he may deserve your loves.
SEC. CIT. Amen, sir: to my poor unworthy notice, 150
He mock'd us when he begg'd our voices.
THIRD CIT. *Certainly*
He flouted us downright.
FIRST CIT. No, 'tis his kind of speech; he did not mock us.
SEC. CIT. Not one amongst us, save yourself, but says
He used us scornfully: he should have show'd us 155
His marks of merit, wounds received for's country.
SIC. Why, so he did, I am sure.
CITIZENS. No, no; no man saw 'em.
THIRD CIT. He said he had wounds which he could show
    in private;

And with his hat, thus waving it in scorn, ₁₆₀
'I would be consul,' says he: 'aged custom,
But by your voices, will not so permit me;
Your voices therefore.' When we granted that,
Here was 'I thank you for your voices: thank you:
Your most sweet voices: now you have left your voices, ₁₆₅
I have no further with you.' Was not this mockery?
SIC. Why, either were you ignorant to see't,
Or, seeing it, of such childish friendliness
To yield your voices?
BRU. Could you not have told him,
As you were lesson'd, when he had no power, ₁₇₀
But was a petty servant to the state,
He was your enemy; ever spake against
Your liberties and the charters that you bear
I' the body of the weal: and now, arriving
A place of potency and sway o' the state, ₁₇₅
If he should still malignantly remain
Fast foe to the plebeii, your voices might
Be curses to yourselves? You should have said,
That as his worthy deeds did claim no less
Than what he stood for, so his gracious nature ₁₈₀
Would think upon you for your voices and
Translate his malice towards you into love,
Standing your friendly lord.
SIC. Thus to have said,
As you were fore-advised, had touch'd his spirit
And tried his inclination; from him pluck'd ₁₈₅
Either his gracious promise, which you might,
As cause had call'd you up, have held him to;
Or else it would have gall'd his surly nature,
Which easily endures not article
Tying him to aught: so, putting him to rage, ₁₉₀
You should have ta'en the advantage of his choler,
And pass'd him unelected.
BRU. Did you perceive
He did solicit you in free contempt
When he did need your loves; and do you think

That his contempt shall not be bruising to you 195
When he hath power to crush? Why, had your bodies
No heart among you? or had you tongues to cry
Against the rectorship of judgement?
SIC. Have you,
Ere now, denied the asker? and now again,
Of him that did not ask but mock, bestow 200
Your sued-for tongues?
THIRD CIT. He's not confirm'd; we may deny him yet.
SEC. CIT. And will deny him:
I'll have five hundred voices of that sound.
FIRST CIT. I twice five hundred, and their friends to piece
    'em. 205
BRU. Get you hence instantly, and tell those friends,
They have chose a consul that will from them take
Their liberties, make them of no more voice
Than dogs that are as often beat for barking
As therefore kept to do so.
SIC. Let them assemble; 210
And, on a safer judgement, all revoke
Your ignorant election: enforce his pride
And his old hate unto you: besides, forget not
With what contempt he wore the humble weed,
How in his suit he scorn'd you: but your loves, 215
Thinking upon his services, took from you
The apprehension of his present portance,
Which most gibingly, ungravely, he did fashion
After the inveterate hate he bears you.
BRU. Lay
A fault on us, your tribunes; that we labour'd, 220
No impediment between, but that you must
Cast your election on him.
SIC. Say, you chose him
More after our commandment than as guided
By your own true affections; and that your minds,
Pre-occupied with what you rather must do 225
Than what you should, made you against the grain
To voice him consul: lay the fault on us.

BRU. Ay, spare us not. Say we read lectures to you,
How youngly he began to serve his country,
How long continued; and what stock he springs of, 230
The noble house o' the Marcians, from whence came
That Ancus Marcius, Numa's daughter's son,
Who, after great Hostilius, here was king;
Of the same house Publius and Quintus were,
That our best water brought by conduits hither; 235
And Censorinus nobly named so,
Twice being by the people chosen censor,
Was his great ancestor.
SIC. One thus descended,
That hath beside well in his person wrought
To be set high in place, we did commend 240
To your remembrances: but you have found,
Scaling his present bearing with his past,
That he's your fixed enemy, and revoke
Your sudden approbation.
BRU. Say, you ne'er had done't—
Harp on that still—but by our putting on: 245
And presently, when you have drawn your number,
Repair to the Capitol.
CITIZENS. We will so: almost all
Repent in their election. (*Exeunt Citizens.*)
BRU. Let them go on;
This mutiny were better put in hazard,
Than stay, past doubt, for greater: 250
If, as his nature is, he fall in rage
With their refusal, both observe and answer
The vantage of his anger.
SIC. To the Capitol, come:
We will be there before the stream o' the people;
And this shall seem, as partly 'tis, their own, 255
Which we have goaded onward. (*Exeunt.*)

ACT III

SCENE I. ROME. A STREET.

(CORNETS. ENTER Coriolanus, Menenius, *ALL THE* Gentry, Cominius, Titus Lartius, *AND OTHER* Senators.)

Cor. Tullus Aufidius then had made new head?
Lart. He had, my lord; and that it was which caused
Our swifter composition.
Cor. So then the Volsces stand but as at first;
Ready, when time shall prompt them, to make road ₅
Upon's again.
Com. They are worn, lord consul, so,
That we shall hardly in our ages see
Their banners wave again.
Cor. Saw you Aufidius?
Lart. On safe-guard he came to me; and did curse
Against the Volsces, for they had so vilely ₁₀
Yielded the town: he is retired to Antium.
Cor. Spoke he of me?
Lart. He did, my lord.
Cor. How? what?
Lart. How often he had met you, sword to sword;

That of all things upon the earth he hated
Your person most; that he would pawn his fortunes 15
To hopeless restitution, so he might
Be call'd your vanquisher.

COR. At Antium lives he?

LART. At Antium.

COR. I wish I had a cause to seek him there,
To oppose his hatred fully. Welcome home. 20
(ENTER SICINIUS AND BRUTUS.)
Behold, these are the tribunes of the people,
The tongues o' the common mouth: I do despise them;
For they do prank them in authority,
Against all noble sufferance.

SIC. Pass no further.

COR. Ha! what is that? 25

BRU. It will be dangerous to go on: no further.

COR. What makes this change?

MEN. The matter?

COM. Hath he not pass'd the noble and the common?

BRU. Cominius, no.

COR. Have I had children's voices? 30

FIRST SEN. Tribunes, give way; he shall to the market-
place.

BRU. The people are incensed against him.

SIC. Stop,
Or all will fall in broil.

COR. Are these your herd?
Must these have voices, that can yield them now,
And straight disclaim their tongues? What are your
offices? 35
You being their mouths, why rule you not their teeth?
Have you not set them on?

MEN. Be calm, be calm.

COR. It is a purposed thing, and grows by plot,
To curb the will of the nobility:
Suffer 't, and live with such as cannot rule, 40
Nor ever will be ruled.

Bru. Call't not a plot:
The people cry you mock'd them; and of late,
When corn was given them gratis, you repined,
Scandal'd the suppliants for the people, call'd them
Time-pleasers, flatterers, foes to nobleness. 45
Cor. Why, this was known before.
Bru. Not to them all.
Cor. Have you inform'd them sithence?
Bru. How! I inform them!
Com. You are like to do such business.
Bru. Not unlike,
Each way, to better yours.
Cor. Why then should I be consul? By yond clouds, 50
Let me deserve so ill as you, and make me
Your fellow tribune.
Sic. You show too much of that
For which the people stir: if you will pass
To where you are bound, you must inquire your way,
Which you are out of, with a gentler spirit; 55
Or never be so noble as a consul,
Nor yoke with him for tribune.
Men. Let's be calm.
Com. The people are abused; set on. This paltering
Becomes not Rome; nor has Coriolanus
Deserved this so dishonour'd rub, laid falsely 60
I' the plain way of his merit.
Cor. Tell me of corn!
This was my speech, and I will speak 't again—
Men. Not now, not now.
First Sen. Not in this heat, sir, now.
Cor. Now, as I live, I will. My nobler friends,
I crave their pardons: 65
For the mutable, rank-scented many, let them
Regard me as I do not flatter, and
Therein behold themselves: I say again,
In soothing them, we nourish 'gainst our senate
The cockle of rebellion, insolence, sedition, 70

Which we ourselves have plough'd for, sow'd and scatter'd,
By mingling them with us, the honour'd number;
Who lack not virtue, no, nor power, but that
Which they have given to beggars.
MEN. Well, no more.
FIRST SEN. No more words, we beseech you.
COR. How! no more! 75
As for my country I have shed my blood,
Not fearing outward force, so shall my lungs
Coin words till their decay against those measles,
Which we disdain should tetter us, yet sought
The very way to catch them.
BRU. You speak o' the people, 80
As if you were a god to punish, not
A man of their infirmity.
SIC. 'Twere well
We let the people know't.
MEN. What, what? his choler?
COR. Choler!
Were I as patient as the midnight sleep, 85
By Jove, 'twould be my mind!
SIC. It is a mind
That shall remain a poison where it is,
Not poison any further.
COR. Shall remain!
Hear you this Triton of the minnows? mark you
His absolute 'shall'?
COM. 'Twas from the canon.
COR. 'Shall'! 90
O good, but most unwise patricians! why,
You grave but reckless senators, have you thus
Given Hydra here to choose an officer,
That with his peremptory 'shall,' being but
The horn and noise o' the monster's, wants not spirit 95
To say he'll turn your current in a ditch,
And make your channel his? If he have power,
Then vail your ignorance; if none, awake
Your dangerous lenity. If you are learn'd,

Be not as common fools; if you are not, 100
Let them have cushions by you. You are plebeians,
If they be senators: and they are no less,
When, both your voices blended, the great'st taste
Most palates theirs. They choose their magistrate;
And such a one as he, who puts his 'shall,' 105
His popular 'shall,' against a graver bench
Than ever frown'd in Greece. By Jove himself,
It makes the consuls base! and my soul aches
To know, when two authorities are up,
Neither supreme, how soon confusion 110
May enter 'twixt the gap of both and take
The one by the other.
Com. Well, on to the market-place.
Cor. Whoever gave that counsel, to give forth
The corn o' the storehouse gratis, as 'twas used
Sometime in Greece,—
Men. Well, well, no more of that. 115
Cor. Though there the people had more absolute power,
I say, they nourish'd disobedience, fed
The ruin of the state.
Bru. Why, shall the people give
One that speaks thus their voice?
Cor. I'll give my reasons,
More worthier than their voices. They know the corn 120
Was not our recompense, resting well assured
They ne'er did service for't: being press'd to the war,
Even when the navel of the state was touch'd,
They would not thread the gates. This kind of service
Did not deserve corn gratis: being i' the war, 125
Their mutinies and revolts, wherein they show'd
Most valour, spoke not for them: the accusation
Which they have often made against the senate,
All cause unborn, could never be the native
Of our so frank donation. Well, what then? 130
How shall this bisson multitude digest
The senate's courtesy? Let deeds express
What's like to be their words: 'We did request it;

We are the greater poll, and in true fear
They gave us our demands.' Thus we debase ₁₃₅
The nature of our seats, and make the rabble
Call our cares fears; which will in time
Break ope the locks o' the senate, and bring in
The crows to peck the eagles.
MEN. Come, enough.
BRU. Enough, with over measure.
COR. No, take more: ₁₄₀
What may be sworn by, both divine and human,
Seal what I end withal! This double worship,
Where one part does disdain with cause, the other
Insult without all reason; where gentry, title, wisdom,
Cannot conclude but by the yea and no ₁₄₅
Of general ignorance,—it must omit
Real necessities, and give way the while
To unstable slightness: purpose so barr'd, it follows,
Nothing is done to purpose. Therefore, beseech you,—
You that will be less fearful than discreet; ₁₅₀
That love the fundamental part of state
More than you doubt the change on 't; that prefer
A noble life before a long, and wish
To jump a body with a dangerous physic
That's sure of death without it,—at once pluck out ₁₅₅
The multitudinous tongue; let them not lick
The sweet which is their poison. Your dishonour
Mangles true judgement and bereaves the state
Of that integrity which should become 't;
Not having the power to do the good it would, ₁₆₀
For the ill which doth control 't.
BRU. Has said enough.
SIC. Has spoken like a traitor, and shall answer
As traitors do.
COR. Thou wretch, despite o'erwhelm thee!
What should the people do with these bald tribunes? ₁₆₅
On whom depending, their obedience fails
To the greater bench: in a rebellion,
When what's not meet, but what must be, was law,

Then were they chosen: in a better hour,
Let what is meet be said it must be meet, 170
And throw their power i' the dust.
BRU. Manifest treason!
SIC. This a consul? no.
BRU. The ædiles, ho!
(Enter an Ædile.)
Let him be apprehended.
SIC. Go, call the people: *(Exit Ædile)* in whose name myself
Attach thee as a traitorous innovator, 175
A foe to the public weal: obey, I charge thee,
And follow to thine answer.
COR. Hence, old goat!
SENATORS, &C. We'll surety him.
COM. Aged sir, hands off.
COR. Hence, rotten thing! or I shall shake thy bones
Out of thy garments.
SIC. Help, ye citizens! 180
(Enter a rabble of Citizens, with the Ædiles.)
MEN. On both sides more respect.
SIC. Here's he that would take from you all your power.
BRU. Seize him, ædiles!
CITIZENS. Down with him! down with him!
SENATORS, &C. Weapons, weapons, weapons! 185
(They all bustle about Coriolanus, crying,)
'Tribunes!' 'Patricians!' 'Citizens!' 'What, ho!'
'Sicinius!' 'Brutus!' 'Coriolanus!' 'Citizens!'
'Peace, peace, peace!' 'Stay! hold! peace!'
MEN. What is about to be? I am out of breath.
Confusion's near. I cannot speak. You, tribunes 190
To the people! Coriolanus, patience!
Speak, good Sicinius.
SIC. Hear me, people; peace!
CITIZENS. Let's hear our tribune: peace!—Speak, speak,
    speak.
SIC. You are at point to lose your liberties:
Marcius would have all from you; Marcius, 195

Whom late you have named for consul.
MEN. Fie, fie, fie!
This is the way to kindle, not to quench.
FIRST SEN. To unbuild the city, and to lay all flat.
SIC. What is the city but the people?
CITIZENS. *True,*
The people are the city. 200
BRU. By the consent of all, we were establish'd
The people's magistrates.
CITIZENS. You so remain.
MEN. And so are like to do.
COM. That is the way to lay the city flat,
To bring the roof to the foundation, 205
And bury all which yet distinctly ranges,
In heaps and piles of ruin.
SIC. This deserves death.
BRU. Or let us stand to our authority,
Or let us lose it. We do here pronounce,
Upon the part o' the people, in whose power 210
We were elected theirs, Marcius is worthy
Of present death.
SIC. Therefore lay hold of him;
Bear him to the rock Tarpeian, and from thence
Into destruction cast him.
BRU. Ædiles, seize him!
CITIZENS. Yield, Marcius, yield!
MEN. Hear me one word; 215
Beseech you, tribunes, hear me but a word.
ÆDILES. Peace, peace!
MEN. (*To Brutus*) Be that you seem, truly your country's
   friend,
And temperately proceed to what you would
Thus violently redress.
BRU. Sir, those cold ways, 220
That seem like prudent helps, are very poisonous
Where the disease is violent. Lay hands upon him,
And bear him to the rock.

COR. *No, I'll die here. (Drawing his sword.)*
There's some among you have beheld me fighting:
Come, try upon yourselves what you have seen me. 225
MEN. Down with that sword! Tribunes, withdraw awhile.
BRU. Lay hands upon him.
MEN. Help Marcius, help,
You that be noble; help him, young and old!
CITIZENS. Down with him, down with him!
(In this mutiny, the Tribunes, the Ædiles, and the People, are beat in.)
MEN. Go, get you to your house; be gone, away! 230
All will be naught else.
SEC. SEN. Get you gone.
COM. Stand fast;
We have as many friends as enemies.
MEN. Shall it be put to that?
FIRST SEN. The gods forbid!
I prithee, noble friend, home to thy house;
Leave us to cure this cause.
MEN. For 'tis a sore upon us 235
You cannot tent yourself: be gone, beseech you.
COM. Come, sir, along with us.
COR. I would they were barbarians—as they are,
Though in Rome litter'd—not Romans—as they are not,
Though calved i' the porch o' the Capitol,—
MEN. Be gone: 240
Put not your worthy rage into your tongue:
One time will owe another.
COR. On fair ground
I could beat forty of them.
MEN. I could myself
Take up a brace o' the best of them; yea, the two tribunes.
COM. But now 'tis odds beyond arithmetic; 245
And manhood is call'd foolery, when it stands
Against a falling fabric. Will you hence
Before the tag return? whose rage doth rend
Like interrupted waters, and o'erbear
What they are used to bear.

MEN. Pray you, be gone: 250
I'll try whether my old wit be in request
With those that have but little: this must be patch'd
With cloth of any colour.
COM. Nay, come away.
(Exeunt Coriolanus, Cominius, and others.)
FIRST PATRICIAN. This man has marr'd his fortune.
MEN. His nature is too noble for the world: 255
He would not flatter Neptune for his trident,
Or Jove for 's power to thunder. His heart's his mouth:
What his breast forges, that his tongue must vent;
And, being angry, does forget that ever
He heard the name of death. *(A noise within.)* 260
Here's goodly work!
SEC. PAT. I would they were a-bed!
MEN. I would they were in Tiber! What, the vengeance,
Could he not speak 'em fair?
(Re-enter BRUTUS and SICINIUS, with the rabble.)
SIC. Where is this viper,
That would depopulate the city, and
Be every man himself?
MEN. You worthy tribunes— 265
SIC. He shall be thrown down the Tarpeian rock
With rigorous hands: he hath resisted law,
And therefore law shall scorn him further trial
Than the severity of the public power,
Which he so sets at nought.
FIRST CIT. He shall well know 270
The noble tribunes are the people's mouths,
And we their hands.
CITIZENS. He shall, sure on't.
MEN. Sir, sir,—
SIC. Peace!
MEN. Do not cry havoc, where you should but hunt 275
With modest warrant.
SIC. Sir, how comes 't that you
Have holp to make this rescue?

MEN. Hear me speak:
As I do know the consul's worthiness,
So can I name his faults,—
SIC. Consul! what consul?
MEN. The consul Coriolanus.
BRU. He consul! 280
CITIZENS. No, no, no, no, no.
MEN. If, by the tribunes' leave, and yours, good people,
I may be heard, I would crave a word or two;
The which shall turn you to no further harm
Than so much loss of time.
SIC. Speak briefly then; 285
For we are peremptory to dispatch
This viperous traitor: to eject him hence
Were but one danger, and to keep him here
Our certain death: therefore it is decreed
He dies to-night.
MEN. Now the good gods forbid 290
That our renowned Rome, whose gratitude
Towards her deserved children is enroll'd
In Jove's own book, like an unnatural dam
Should now eat up her own!
SIC. He's a disease that must be cut away. 295
MEN. O, he's a limb that has but a disease;
Mortal, to cut it off; to cure it, easy.
What has he done to Rome that's worthy death?
Killing our enemies, the blood he hath lost—
Which, I dare vouch, is more than that he hath 300
By many an ounce—he dropp'd it for his country;
And what is left, to lose it by his country
Were to us all that do 't and suffer it
A brand to the end o' the world.
SIC. This is clean kam.
BRU. Merely awry: when he did love his country, 305
It honour'd him.
MEN. The service of the foot
Being once gangrened, is not then respected
For what before it was.

Bru. We'll hear no more.
Pursue him to his house, and pluck him thence;
Lest his infection, being of catching nature, ₃₁₀
Spread further.
Men. One word more, one word.
This tiger-footed rage, when it shall find
The harm of unscann'd swiftness, will, too late,
Tie leaden pounds to 's heels. Proceed by process;
Lest parties, as he is beloved, break out, ₃₁₅
And sack great Rome with Romans.
Bru. If it were so—
Sic. What do ye talk?
Have we not had a taste of his obedience?
Our ædiles smote? ourselves resisted? Come.
Men. Consider this: he has been bred i' the wars ₃₂₀
Since he could draw a sword, and is ill school'd
In bolted language; meal and bran together
He throws without distinction. Give me leave,
I'll go to him, and undertake to bring him
Where he shall answer, by a lawful form, ₃₂₅
In peace, to his utmost peril.
First Sen. Noble tribunes,
It is the humane way: the other course
Will prove too bloody; and the end of it
Unknown to the beginning.
Sic. Noble Menenius,
Be you then as the people's officer. ₃₃₀
Masters, lay down your weapons.
Bru. Go not home.
Sic. Meet on the market-place. We'll attend you there:
Where, if you bring not Marcius, we'll proceed
In our first way.
Men. I'll bring him to you.
(*To the Senators*) Let me desire your company: he must
      come, ₃₃₅
Or what is worst will follow.
First Sen. Pray you, let's to him. (*Exeunt.*)

SCENE II. A ROOM IN CORIOLANUS'S HOUSE

(Enter Coriolanus *with* Patricians.*)*

Cor. Let them pull all about mine ears; present me
Death on the wheel, or at wild horses' heels;
Or pile ten hills on the Tarpeian rock,
That the precipitation might down stretch
Below the beam of sight; yet will I still 5
Be thus to them.
A Patrician. You do the nobler.
Cor. I muse my mother
Does not approve me further, who was wont
To call them woollen vassals, things created
To buy and sell with groats, to show bare heads 10
In congregations, to yawn, be still and wonder,
When one but of my ordinance stood up
To speak of peace or war.
(Enter Volumnia.*)*
I talk of you:
Why did you wish me milder? would you have me
False to my nature? Rather say, I play 15
The man I am.
Vol. O, sir, sir, sir,
I would have had you put your power well on,
Before you had worn it out.
Cor. Let go.
Vol. You might have been enough the man you are,
With striving less to be so: lesser had been 20
The thwartings of your dispositions, if
You had not show'd them how ye were disposed
Ere they lack'd power to cross you.
Cor. Let them hang.
Vol. Ay, and burn too.
(Enter Menenius *with the Senators.)*
Men. Come, come, you have been too rough, something
too rough;25

You must return and mend it.
FIRST SEN. There's no remedy;
Unless, by not so doing, our good city
Cleave in the midst, and perish.
VOL. Pray, be counsell'd:
I have a heart as little apt as yours,
But yet a brain that leads my use of anger 30
To better vantage.
MEN. Well said, noble woman!
Before he should thus stoop to the herd, but that
The violent fit o' the time craves it as physic
For the whole state, I would put mine armour on,
Which I can scarcely bear.
COR. What must I do? 35
MEN. Return to the tribunes.
COR. Well, what then? what then?
MEN. Repent what you have spoke.
COR. For them! I cannot do it to the gods;
Must I then do't to them?
VOL. You are too absolute;
Though therein you can never be too noble, 40
But when extremities speak. I have heard you say,
Honour and policy, like unsever'd friends,
I' the war do grow together: grant that, and tell me,
In peace what each of them by the other lose,
That they combine not there.
COR. Tush, tush!
MEN. A good demand. 45
VOL. If it be honour in your wars to seem
The same you are not, which, for your best ends,
You adopt your policy, how is it less or worse,
That it shall hold companionship in peace
With honour, as in war, since that to both 50
It stands in like request?
COR. Why force you this?
VOL. Because that now it lies you on to speak
To the people; not by your own instruction,

Nor by the matter which your heart prompts you,
But with such words that are but roted in 55
Your tongue, though but bastards and syllables
Of no allowance to your bosom's truth.
Now, this no more dishonours you at all
Than to take in a town with gentle words,
Which else would put you to your fortune and 60
The hazard of much blood.
I would dissemble with my nature, where
My fortunes and my friends at stake required
I should do so in honour. I am in this,
Your wife, your son, these senators, the nobles; 65
And you will rather show our general louts
How you can frown than spend a fawn upon 'em,
For the inheritance of their loves and safeguard
Of what that want might ruin.

MEN. Noble lady!
Come, go with us; speak fair: you may salve so, 70
Not what is dangerous present, but the loss
Of what is past.

VOL. I prithee now, my son,
Go to them, with this bonnet in thy hand;
And thus far having stretch'd it—here be with them—
Thy knee bussing the stones—for in such business 75
Action is eloquence, and the eyes of the ignorant
More learned than the ears—waving thy head,
Which often, thus, correcting thy stout heart,
Now humble as the ripest mulberry
That will not hold the handling: or say to them, 80
Thou art their soldier, and being bred in broils
Hast not the soft way which, thou dost confess,
Were fit for thee to use, as they to claim,
In asking their good loves; but thou wilt frame
Thyself, forsooth, hereafter theirs, so far 85
As thou hast power and person.

MEN. This but done,
Even as she speaks, why, their hearts were yours;
For they have pardons, being ask'd, as free

As words to little purpose.

VOL. Prithee now,
Go, and be ruled: although I know thou hadst rather ₉₀
Follow thine enemy in a fiery gulf
Than flatter him in a bower.

(ENTER COMINIUS.)

Here is Cominius.

COM. I have been i' the market-place; and, sir, 'tis fit
You make strong party, or defend yourself
By calmness or by absence: all's in anger. ₉₅

MEN. Only fair speech.

COM. I think 'twill serve, if he
Can thereto frame his spirit.

VOL. He must, and will.
Prithee now, say you will, and go about it.

COR. Must I go show them my unbarb'd sconce? must I,
With my base tongue, give to my noble heart ₁₀₀
A lie, that it must bear? Well, I will do't:
Yet, were there but this single plot to lose,
This mould of Marcius, they to dust should grind it,
And throw't against the wind. To the market-place!
You have put me now to such a part, which never ₁₀₅
I shall discharge to the life.

COM. Come, come, we'll prompt you.

VOL. I prithee now, sweet son, as thou hast said
My praises made thee first a soldier, so,
To have my praise for this, perform a part
Thou hast not done before.

COR. Well, I must do't: ₁₁₀
Away, my disposition, and possess me
Some harlot's spirit! my throat of war be turn'd,
Which quired with my drum, into a pipe
Small as an eunuch, or the virgin voice
That babies lulls asleep! the smiles of knaves ₁₁₅
Tent in my cheeks, and schoolboys' tears take up
The glasses of my sight! a beggar's tongue
Make motion through my lips, and my arm'd knees,
Who bow'd but in my stirrup, bend like his

That hath received an alms! I will not do't; ₁₂₀
Lest I surcease to honour mine own truth,
And by my body's action teach my mind
A most inherent baseness.

VOL. At thy choice then:
To beg of thee, it is my more dishonour
Than thou of them. Come all to ruin: let ₁₂₅
Thy mother rather feel thy pride than fear
Thy dangerous stoutness, for I mock at death
With as big heart as thou. Do as thou list.
Thy valiantness was mine, thou suck'dst it from me,
But owe thy pride thyself.

COR. Pray, be content: ₁₃₀
Mother, I am going to the market-place;
Chide me no more. I'll mountebank their loves,
Cog their hearts from them and come home beloved
Of all the trades in Rome. Look, I am going:
Commend me to my wife. I'll return consul; ₁₃₅
Or never trust to what my tongue can do
I' the way of flattery further.

VOL. Do your will. (*Exit.*)

COM. Away! the tribunes do attend you: arm yourself
To answer mildly; for they are prepared
With accusations, as I hear, more strong ₁₄₀
Than are upon you yet.

COR. The word is 'mildly.' Pray you, let us go:
Let them accuse me by invention, I
Will answer in mine honour.

MEN. Ay, but mildly.

COR. Well, mildly be it then. Mildly! (*Exeunt.*) ₁₄₅

SCENE III. THE SAME. THE FORUM

(*ENTER* SICINIUS *AND* BRUTUS.)

BRU. In this point charge him home, that he affects
Tyrannical power: if he evade us there,

Enforce him with his envy to the people;
And that the spoil got on the Antiates
Was ne'er distributed. 5
(Enter an Ædile.)
What, will he come?
Æd. He's coming.
Bru. How accompanied?
Æd. With old Menenius and those senators
That always favour'd him.
Sic. Have you a catalogue
Of all the voices that we have procured,
Set down by the poll?
Æd. I have; 'tis ready. 10
Sic. Have you collected them by tribes?
Æd. I have.
Sic. Assemble presently the people hither:
And when they hear me say 'It shall be so
I' the right and strength o' the commons,' be it either
For death, for fine, or banishment, then let them, 15
If I say fine, cry 'Fine,' if death, cry 'Death,'
Insisting on the old prerogative
And power i' the truth o' the cause.
Æd. I shall inform them.
Bru. And when such time they have begun to cry,
Let them not cease, but with a din confused 20
Enforce the present execution
Of what we chance to sentence.
Æd. Very well.
Sic. Make them be strong, and ready for this hint,
When we shall hap to give't them.
Bru. *Go about it. (Exit Ædile.)*
Put him to choler straight: he hath been used 25
Ever to conquer and to have his worth
Of contradiction: being once chafed, he cannot
Be rein'd again to temperance; then he speaks
What's in his heart; and that is there which looks
With us to break his neck.

Sic. Well, here he comes. 30

(Enter Coriolanus, Menenius, *and* Cominius, *with* Senators *and* Patricians.)

Men. Calmly, I do beseech you.

Cor. Ay, as an ostler, that for the poorest piece
Will bear the knave by the volume. The honour'd gods
Keep Rome in safety, and the chairs of justice
Supplied with worthy men! plant love among's! 35
Throng our large temples with the shows of peace,
And not our streets with war!

First Sen. Amen, amen.

Men. A noble wish.

(Re-enter Ædile, *with* Citizens.)

Sic. Draw near, ye people.

Æd. List to your tribunes; audience: peace, I say! 40

Cor. First, hear me speak.

Both Tri. Well, say. Peace, ho!

Cor. Shall I be charged no further than this present?
Must all determine here?

Sic. I do demand,
If you submit you to the people's voices,
Allow their officers, and are content 45
To suffer lawful censure for such faults
As shall be proved upon you?

Cor. I am content.

Men. Lo, citizens, he says he is content:
The warlike service he has done, consider; think
Upon the wounds his body bears, which show 50
Like graves i' the holy churchyard.

Cor. Scratches with briers,
Scars to move laughter only.

Men. Consider further,
That when he speaks not like a citizen,
You find him like a soldier: do not take
His rougher accents for malicious sounds, 55
But, as I say, such as become a soldier
Rather than envy you.

Com. Well, well, no more.

Cor. What is the matter
That being pass'd for consul with full voice,
I am so dishonour'd that the very hour 60
You take it off again?

Sic. Answer to us.

Cor. Say, then: 'tis true, I ought so.

Sic. We charge you, that you have contrived to take
From Rome all season'd office and to wind
Yourself into a power tyrannical; 65
For which you are a traitor to the people.

Cor. How! traitor!

Men. Nay, temperately; your promise.

Cor. The fires i' the lowest hell fold-in the people!
Call me their traitor! Thou injurious tribune!
Within thine eyes sat twenty thousand deaths, 70
In thy hands clutch'd as many millions, in
Thy lying tongue both numbers, I would say
'Thou liest' unto thee with a voice as free
As I do pray the gods.

Sic. Mark you this, people?

Citizens. To the rock, to the rock with him!

Sic. Peace! 75
We need not put new matter to his charge:
What you have seen him do and heard him speak,
Beating your officers, cursing yourselves,
Opposing laws with strokes, and here defying
Those whose great power must try him; even this, 80
So criminal and in such capital kind,
Deserves the extremest death.

Bru. But since he hath
Served well for Rome—

Cor. What do you prate of service?

Bru. I talk of that, that know it.

Cor. You? 85

Men. Is this the promise that you made your mother?

Com. Know, I pray you,—

COR. I'll know no further:
Let them pronounce the steep Tarpeian death,
Vagabond exile, flaying, pent to linger
But with a grain a day, I would not buy 90
Their mercy at the price of one fair word,
Nor check my courage for what they can give,
To have't with saying 'Good morrow.'
SIC. For that he has,
As much as in him lies, from time to time
Envied against the people, seeking means 95
To pluck away their power, as now at last
Given hostile strokes, and that not in the presence
Of dreaded justice, but on the ministers
That do distribute it; in the name o' the people,
And in the power of us the tribunes, we, 100
Even from this instant, banish him our city,
In peril of precipitation
From off the rock Tarpeian, never more
To enter our Rome gates: i' the people's name,
I say it shall be so. 105
CITIZENS. It shall be so, it shall be so; let him away:
He's banish'd, and it shall be so.
COM. Hear me, my masters, and my common friends,—
SIC. He's sentenced; no more hearing.
COM. Let me speak:
I have been consul, and can show for Rome 110
Her enemies' marks upon me. I do love
My country's good with a respect more tender,
More holy and profound, than mine own life,
My dear wife's estimate, her womb's increase
And treasure of my loins; then if I would 115
Speak that—
SIC. We know your drift:—speak what?
BRU. There's no more to be said, but he is banish'd,
As enemy to the people and his country:
It shall be so.
CITIZENS. It shall be so, it shall be so. 120
COR. You common cry of curs! whose breath I hate

As reek o' the rotten fens, whose loves I prize
As the dead carcasses of unburied men
That do corrupt my air, I banish you;
And here remain with your uncertainty! 125
Let every feeble rumour shake your hearts!
Your enemies, with nodding of their plumes,
Fan you into despair! Have the power still
To banish your defenders; till at length
Your ignorance, which finds not till it feels, 130
Making not reservation of yourselves,
Still your own foes, deliver you as most
Abated captives to some nation
That won you without blows! Despising,
For you, the city, thus I turn my back: 135
There is a world elsewhere.
(Exeunt Coriolanus, Cominius, Menenius, Senators and Patricians.)
Æd. The people's enemy is gone, is gone!
Citizens. Our enemy is banish'd! he is gone! Hoo! hoo!
(They all shout, and throw up their caps.)
Sic. Go, see him out at gates, and follow him,
As he hath follow'd you, with all despite; 140
Give him deserved vexation. Let a guard
Attend us through the city.
Citizens. Come, come, let's see him out at gates; come.
The gods preserve our noble tribunes! Come. *(Exeunt.)*

ACT IV

SCENE I. ROME. BEFORE A GATE OF THE CITY.

(ENTER CORIOLANUS, VOLUMNIA, VIRGILIA, MENENIUS, COMINIUS, WITH THE YOUNG NOBILITY OF ROME.)

COR. Come, leave your tears; a brief farewell: the beast
With many heads butts me away. Nay, mother,
Where is your ancient courage? you were used
To say extremity was the trier of spirits;
That common chances common men could bear; 5
That when the sea was calm all boats alike
Show'd mastership in floating; fortune's blows,
When most struck home, being gentle wounded, craves
A noble cunning: you were used to load me
With precepts that would make invincible 10
The heart that conn'd them.
VIR. O heavens! O heavens!
COR. Nay, I prithee, woman,—
VOL. Now the red pestilence strike all trades in Rome,
And occupations perish!
COR. What, what, what!
I shall be loved when I am lack'd. Nay, mother, 15

Resume that spirit, when you were wont to say,
If you had been the wife of Hercules,
Six of his labours you'ld have done, and saved
Your husband so much sweat. Cominius,
Droop not; adieu. Farewell, my wife, my mother: 20
I'll do well yet. Thou old and true Menenius,
Thy tears are salter than a younger man's,
And venomous to thine eyes. My sometime general,
I have seen thee stern, and thou hast oft beheld
Heart-hardening spectacles; tell these sad women, 25
'Tis fond to wail inevitable strokes,
As 'tis to laugh at 'em. My mother, you wot well
My hazards still have been your solace: and
Believe 't not lightly—though I go alone,
Like to a lonely dragon, that his fen 30
Makes fear'd and talk'd of more than seen—your son
Will or exceed the common, or be caught
With cautelous baits and practice.
VOL. My first son,
Whither wilt thou go? Take good Cominius
With thee awhile: determine on some course, 35
More than a wild exposture to each chance
That starts i' the way before thee.
COR. O the gods!
COM. I'll follow thee a month, devise with thee
Where thou shalt rest, that thou mayst hear of us
And we of thee: so, if the time thrust forth 40
A cause for thy repeal, we shall not send
O'er the vast world to seek a single man,
And lose advantage, which doth ever cool
I' the absence of the needer.
COR. Fare ye well:
Thou hast years upon thee; and thou art too full 45
Of the wars' surfeits, to go rove with one
That's yet unbruised: bring me but out at gate.
Come, my sweet wife, my dearest mother, and
My friends of noble touch, when I am forth,
Bid me farewell, and smile. I pray you, come. 50

While I remain above the ground, you shall
Hear from me still, and never of me aught
But what is like me formerly.
MEN. That's worthily
As any ear can hear. Come, let's not weep.
If I could shake off but one seven years 55
From these old arms and legs, by the good gods,
I'ld with thee every foot.
COR. Give me thy hand:
Come. (*Exeunt.*)

SCENE II. THE SAME. A STREET NEAR THE GATE.

(Enter the two Tribunes, SICINIUS and BRUTUS, with the Ædile.)

SIC. Bid them all home; he's gone, and we'll no further.
The nobility are vex'd, whom we see have sided
In his behalf.
BRU. Now we have shown our power,
Let us seem humbler after it is done
Than when it was a-doing.
SIC. Bid them home: 5
Say their great enemy is gone and they
Stand in their ancient strength.
BRU. Dismiss them home. (*Exit Ædile.*)
Here comes his mother.
(ENTER VOLUMNIA, VIRGILIA, AND MENENIUS.)
SIC. Let's not meet her.
BRU. Why?
SIC. They say she's mad.
BRU. They have ta'en note of us: keep on your way. 10
VOL. O, ye're well met: the hoarded plague o' the gods
Requite your love!
MEN. Peace, peace; be not so loud.
VOL. If that I could for weeping, you should hear,—
Nay, and you shall hear some. (*To Brutus*) Will you be
    gone?

VIR. (*To Sicinius*) You shall stay too: I would I had the
power₁₅
To say so to my husband.

SIC. Are you mankind?

VOL. Ay, fool; is that a shame? Note but this fool.
Was not a man my father? Hadst thou foxship
To banish him that struck more blows for Rome
Than thou hast spoken words?

SIC. O blessed heavens! ₂₀

VOL. Moe noble blows than ever thou wise words;
And for Rome's good. I'll tell thee what; yet go:
Nay, but thou shalt stay too: I would my son
Were in Arabia, and thy tribe before him,
His good sword in his hand.

SIC. What then?

VIR. What then! ₂₅
He'ld make an end of thy posterity.

VOL. Bastards and all.
Good man, the wounds that he does bear for Rome!

MEN. Come, come, peace.

SIC. I would he had continued to his country ₃₀
As he began, and not unknit himself
The noble knot he made.

BRU. I would he had.

VOL. 'I would he had!' 'Twas you incensed the rabble;
Cats, that can judge as fitly of his worth
As I can of those mysteries which heaven ₃₅
Will not have earth to know.

BRU. Pray, let us go.

VOL. Now, pray, sir, get you gone:
You have done a brave deed. Ere you go, hear this:
As far as doth the Capitol exceed
The meanest house in Rome, so far my son— ₄₀
This lady's husband here, this, do you see?—
Whom you have banish'd, does exceed you all.

BRU. Well, well, we'll leave you.

SIC. Why stay we to be baited

With one that wants her wits?
VOL. Take my prayers with you.
(Exeunt Tribunes.)
I would the gods had nothing else to do ₄₅
But to confirm my curses! Could I meet 'em
But once a-day, it would unclog my heart
Of what lies heavy to 't.
MEN. You have told them home;
And, by my troth, you have cause. You'll sup with me?
VOL. Anger's my meat; I sup upon myself, ₅₀
And so shall starve with feeding. Come, let's go:
Leave this faint puling, and lament as I do,
In anger, Juno-like. Come, come, come.
(Exeunt Vol. and Vir.)
MEN. Fie, fie, fie! *(Exit.)*

SCENE III. A HIGHWAY BETWEEN ROME AND ANTIUM.

(Enter a Roman and a Volsce, meeting.)

ROM. I know you well, sir, and you know me: your
name, I think, is Adrian.
VOLS. It is so, sir: truly, I have forgot you.
ROM. I am a Roman; and my services are, as you are,
against 'em: know you me yet? ₅
VOLS. Nicanor? no.
ROM. The same, sir.
VOLS. You had more beard when I last saw you; but
your favour is well appeared by your tongue. What's the
news in Rome? I have a note from the Volscian state, to ₁₀
find you out there: you have well saved me a day's journey.
ROM. There hath been in Rome strange insurrections;
the people against the senators, patricians and nobles.
VOLS. Hath been! is it ended then? Our state thinks
not so: they are in a most warlike preparation, and hope ₁₅
to come upon them in the heat of their division.

Rom. The main blaze of it is past, but a small thing
would make it flame again: for the nobles receive so to
heart the banishment of that worthy Coriolanus, that they
are in a ripe aptness to take all power from the people
    and 20
to pluck from them their tribunes for ever. This lies
    glowing,
I can tell you, and is almost mature for the violent
breaking out.

Vols. Coriolanus banished!

Rom. Banished, sir. 25

Vols. You will be welcome with this intelligence,
Nicanor.

Rom. The day serves well for them now. I have heard
it said, the fittest time to corrupt a man's wife is when she's
fallen out with her husband. Your noble Tullus Aufidius 30
will appear well in these wars, his great opposer,
    Coriolanus,
being now in no request of his country.

Vols. He cannot choose. I am most fortunate, thus
accidentally to encounter you: you have ended my business,
and I will merrily accompany you home. 35

Rom. I shall, between this and supper, tell you most
strange things from Rome; all tending to the good of their
adversaries. Have you an army ready, say you?

Vols. A most royal one; the centurions and their
charges, distinctly billeted, already in the entertainment, 40
and to be on foot at an hour's warning.

Rom. I am joyful to hear of their readiness, and am
the man, I think, that shall set them in present action. So,
sir, heartily well met, and most glad of your company.

Vols. You take my part from me, sir; I have the most 45
cause to be glad of yours.

Rom. Well, let us go together. (*Exeunt.*)

SCENE IV. ANTIUM. BEFORE AUFIDIUS'S HOUSE

(Enter CORIOLANUS in mean apparel, disguised and muffled.)

COR. A goodly city is this Antium. City,
'Tis I that made thy widows: many an heir
Of these fair edifices 'fore my wars
Have I heard groan and drop: then know me not;
Lest that thy wives with spits, and boys with stones, 5
In puny battle slay me.
(Enter a Citizen.)
Save you, sir.
CIT. And you.
COR. Direct me, if it be your will,
Where great Aufidius lies: is he in Antium?
CIT. He is, and feasts the nobles of the state
At his house this night.
COR. Which is his house, beseech you? 10
CIT. This, here, before you.
COR. Thank you, sir: farewell.
(Exit Citizen.)
O world, thy slippery turns! Friends now fast sworn,
Whose double bosoms seem to wear one heart,
Whose hours, whose bed, whose meal and exercise
Are still together, who twin, as 'twere, in love 15
Unseparable, shall within this hour,
On a dissension of a doit, break out
To bitterest enmity: so, fellest foes,
Whose passions and whose plots have broke their sleep
To take the one the other, by some chance, 20
Some trick not worth an egg, shall grow dear friends
And interjoin their issues. So with me:
My birth-place hate I, and my love's upon
This enemy town. I'll enter: if he slay me,
He does fair justice; if he give me way, 25
I'll do his country service. *(Exit.)*

SCENE V. THE SAME. A HALL IN AUFIDIUS'S HOUSE.

(Music within. Enter a Servingman.)

FIRST SERV. Wine, wine, wine!—What service is here!
I think our fellows are asleep. *(Exit.)*
(Enter another Servingman.)
SEC. SERV. Where's Cotus? my master calls for him.
Cotus! *(Exit.)*
(ENTER CORIOLANUS.)
COR. A goodly house: the feast smells well; but I ₅
Appear not like a guest.
(Re-enter the first Servingman.)
FIRST SERV. What would you have, friend? whence are
you? Here's no place for you: pray, go to the door. *(Exit.)*
COR. I have deserved no better entertainment,
In being Coriolanus. ₁₀
(Re-enter second Servingman.)
SEC. SERV. Whence are you, sir? Has the porter his
eyes in his head, that he gives entrance to such
    companions?
Pray, get you out.
COR. Away!
SEC. SERV. 'Away!' get you away. ₁₅
COR. Now thou'rt troublesome.
SEC. SERV. Are you so brave? I'll have you talked
with anon.
(Enter a third Servingman. The first meets him.)
THIRD SERV. What fellow's this?
FIRST SERV. A strange one as ever I looked on: I cannot ₂₀
get him out o' the house: prithee, call my master to him.
(Retires.)
THIRD SERV. What have you to do here, fellow? Pray
you, avoid the house.
COR. Let me but stand; I will not hurt your hearth.
THIRD SERV. What are you? ₂₅

COR. A gentleman.

THIRD SERV. A marvellous poor one.

COR. True, so I am.

THIRD SERV. Pray you, poor gentleman, take up some
other station; here's no place for you; pray you, avoid: 30
come.

COR. Follow your function, go, and batten on cold bits.
(Pushes him away from him.)

THIRD SERV. What, you will not? Prithee, tell my
master what a strange guest he has here.

SEC. SERV. And I shall. *(Exit.)* 35

THIRD SERV. Where dwell'st thou?

COR. Under the canopy.

THIRD SERV. Under the canopy!

COR. Ay.

THIRD SERV. Where's that? 40

COR. I' the city of kites and crows.

THIRD SERV. I' the city of kites and crows! What an
ass it is! Then thou dwell'st with daws too?

COR. No, I serve not thy master.

THIRD SERV. How, sir! do you meddle with my master? 45

COR. Ay; 'tis an honester service than to meddle with
thy mistress:

Thou pratest, and pratest; serve with thy trencher, hence!
(Beats him away. Exit third Servingman.)
(Enter AUFIDIUS with the second Servingman.)

AUF. Where is this fellow?

SEC. SERV. Here, sir: I'ld have beaten him like a dog, 50
but for disturbing the lords within. *(Retires.)*

AUF. Whence comest thou? what wouldst thou? thy name?
Why speak'st not? speak, man: what's thy name?

COR. *(Unmuffling)* If, Tullus,
Not yet thou knowest me, and, seeing me, dost not
Think me for the man I am, necessity 55
Commands me name myself.

AUF. What is thy name?

COR. A name unmusical to the Volscians' ears,

And harsh in sound to thine.
AUF. Say, what's thy name?
Thou hast a grim appearance, and thy face
Bears a command in 't; though thy tackle's torn, 60
Thou show'st a noble vessel: what's thy name?
COR. Prepare thy brow to frown:—know'st thou me yet?
AUF. I know thee not:—thy name?
COR. My name is Caius Marcius, who hath done
To thee particularly, and to all the Volsces, 65
Great hurt and mischief; thereto witness may
My surname, Coriolanus: the painful service,
The extreme dangers, and the drops of blood
Shed for my thankless country, are requited
But with that surname; a good memory, 70
And witness of the malice and displeasure
Which thou shouldst bear me: only that name remains:
The cruelty and envy of the people,
Permitted by our dastard nobles, who
Have all forsook me, hath devour'd the rest; 75
And suffer'd me by the voice of slaves to be
Whoop'd out of Rome. Now, this extremity
Hath brought me to thy hearth: not out of hope—
Mistake me not—to save my life, for if
I had fear'd death, of all the men i' the world 80
I would have 'voided thee; but in mere spite,
To be full quit of those my banishers,
Stand I before thee here. Then if thou hast
A heart of wreak in thee, that wilt revenge
Thine own particular wrongs and stop those maims 85
Of shame seen through thy country, speed thee straight,
And make my misery serve thy turn: so use it
That my revengeful services may prove
As benefits to thee; for I will fight
Against my canker'd country with the spleen 90
Of all the under fiends. But if so be
Thou darest not this and that to prove more fortunes
Thou'rt tired, then, in a word, I also am
Longer to live most weary, and present

My throat to thee and to thy ancient malice; 95
Which not to cut would show thee but a fool,
Since I have ever follow'd thee with hate,
Drawn tuns of blood out of thy country's breast,
And cannot live but to thy shame, unless
It be to do thee service.
Auf. O Marcius, Marcius! 100
Each word thou hast spoke hath weeded from my heart
A root of ancient envy. If Jupiter
Should from yond cloud speak divine things,
And say 'Tis true,' I'ld not believe them more
Than thee, all noble Marcius. Let me twine 105
Mine arms about that body, where against
My grained ash an hundred times hath broke,
And scarr'd the moon with splinters: here I clip
The anvil of my sword, and do contest
As hotly and as nobly with thy love 110
As ever in ambitious strength I did
Contend against thy valour. Know thou first,
I loved the maid I married; never man
Sigh'd truer breath; but that I see thee here,
Thou noble thing! more dances my rapt heart 115
Than when I first my wedded mistress saw
Bestride my threshold. Why, thou Mars! I tell thee,
We have a power on foot; and I had purpose
Once more to hew thy target from thy brawn,
Or lose mine arm for't: thou hast beat me out 120
Twelve several times, and I have nightly since
Dreamt of encounters 'twixt thyself and me;
We have been down together in my sleep,
Unbuckling helms, fisting each other's throat;
And waked half dead with nothing. Worthy Marcius, 125
Had we no quarrel else to Rome but that
Thou art thence banish'd, we would muster all
From twelve to seventy, and pouring war
Into the bowels of ungrateful Rome,
Like a bold flood o'er-beat. O, come, go in, 130
And take our friendly senators by the hands,

Who now are here, taking their leaves of me,
Who am prepared against your territories,
Though not for Rome itself.

COR. You bless me, gods!

AUF. Therefore, most absolute sir, if thou wilt have 135
The leading of thine own revenges, take
The one half of my commission, and set down—
As best thou art experienced, since thou know'st
Thy country's strength and weakness—thine own ways;
Whether to knock against the gates of Rome, 140
Or rudely visit them in parts remote,
To fright them, ere destroy. But come in:
Let me commend thee first to those that shall
Say yea to thy desires. A thousand welcomes!
And more a friend than e'er an enemy; 145
Yet, Marcius, that was much. Your hand: most welcome!

*(Exeunt Coriolanus and Aufidius. The two Servingmen come
    forward.)*

FIRST SERV. Here's a strange alteration!

SEC. SERV. By my hand, I had thought to have strucken
him with a cudgel; and yet my mind gave me his clothes
made a false report of him. 150

FIRST SERV. What an arm he has! he turned me about
with his finger and his thumb, as one would set up a top.

SEC. SERV. Nay, I knew by his face that there was
something in him: he had, sir, a kind of face, methought,
    —I
cannot tell how to term it. 155

FIRST SERV. He had so; looking as it were—Would I
were hanged, but I thought there was more in him than I
could think.

SEC. SERV. So did I, I'll be sworn: he is simply the
rarest man i' the world. 160

FIRST SERV. I think he is: but a greater soldier than
he, you wot one.

SEC. SERV. Who? my master?

FIRST SERV. Nay, it's no matter for that.

SEC. SERV. Worth six on him. ₁₆₅

FIRST SERV. Nay, not so neither: but I take him to be the greater soldier.

SEC. SERV. Faith, look you, one cannot tell how to say that: for the defence of a town, our general is excellent.

FIRST SERV. Ay, and for an assault too. ₁₇₀

(Re-enter third Servingman.)

THIRD SERV. O slaves, I can tell you news; news, you rascals!

FIRST AND SEC. SERV. What, what, what? let's partake.

THIRD SERV. I would not be a Roman, of all nations; I had as lieve be a condemned man. ₁₇₅

FIRST AND SEC. SERV. Wherefore? wherefore?

THIRD SERV. Why, here's he that was wont to thwack our general, Caius Marcius.

FIRST SERV. Why do you say, thwack our general?

THIRD SERV. I do not say, thwack our general; but he ₁₈₀ was always good enough for him.

SEC. SERV. Come, we are fellows and friends: he was ever too hard for him; I have heard him say so himself.

FIRST SERV. He was too hard for him directly, to say the troth on 't: before Corioli he scotched him and notched ₁₈₅
him like a carbonado.

SEC. SERV. An he had been cannibally given, he might have broiled and eaten him too.

FIRST SERV. But, more of thy news?

THIRD SERV. Why, he is so made on here within as if ₁₉₀ he were son and heir to Mars; set at upper end o' the table; no question asked him by any of the senators, but they stand bald before him. Our general himself makes a mistress of him; sanctifies himself with 's hand, and turns up the white o' the eye to his discourse. But the bottom of ₁₉₅
the news is, our general is cut i' the middle, and but one half of what he was yesterday; for the other has half, by the entreaty and grant of the whole table. He'll go, he

says, and sowl the porter of Rome gates by the ears: he will mow all down before him, and leave his passage poll'd. 200

Sec. Serv. And he's as like to do't as any man I can imagine.

Third Serv. Do't! he will do't; for, look you, sir, he has as many friends as enemies; which friends, sir, as it were, durst not, look you, sir, show themselves, as we term 205 it, his friends whilst he's in directitude.

First Serv. Directitude! what's that?

Third Serv. But when they shall see, sir, his crest up again and the man in blood, they will out of their burrows, like conies after rain, and revel all with him. 210

First Serv. But when goes this forward?

Third Serv. To-morrow; to-day; presently: you shall have the drum struck up this afternoon: 'tis, as it were, a parcel of their feast, and to be executed ere they wipe their lips. 215

Sec. Serv. Why, then we shall have a stirring world again. This peace is nothing, but to rust iron, increase tailors and breed ballad-makers.

First Serv. Let me have war, say I; it exceeds peace as far as day does night; it's spritely, waking, audible, and 220 full of vent. Peace is a very apoplexy, lethargy, mull'd, deaf, sleepy, insensible; a getter of more bastard children than war's a destroyer of men.

Sec. Serv. 'Tis so: and as war, in some sort, may be said to be a ravisher, so it cannot be denied but peace is a 225 great maker of cuckolds.

First Serv. Ay, and it makes men hate one another.

Third Serv. Reason; because they then less need one another. The wars for my money. I hope to see Romans as cheap as Volscians. They are rising, they are rising. 230

First and Sec. Serv. *In, in, in, in! (Exeunt.)*

SCENE VI. ROME. A PUBLIC PLACE

(Enter the two Tribunes, SICINIUS and BRUTUS.)

SIC. We hear not of him, neither need we fear him;
His remedies are tame i' the present peace
And quietness of the people, which before
Were in wild hurry. Here do we make his friends
Blush that the world goes well; who rather had, 5
Though they themselves did suffer by't, behold
Dissentious numbers pestering streets than see
Our tradesmen singing in their shops and going
About their functions friendly.
BRU. We stood to 't in good time.
(ENTER MENENIUS.)
Is this Menenius? 10
SIC. 'Tis he, 'tis he: O, he is grown most kind
Of late. Hail, sir!
MEN. Hail to you both!
SIC. Your Coriolanus is not much miss'd,
But with his friends: the commonwealth doth stand;
And so would do, were he more angry at it. 15
MEN. All's well; and might have been much better, if
He could have temporized.
SIC. Where is he, hear you?
MEN. Nay, I hear nothing: his mother and his wife
Hear nothing from him.
(Enter three or four Citizens.)
CITIZENS. The gods preserve you both!
SIC. God-den, our neighbours. 20
BRU. God-den to you all, god-den to you all.
FIRST CIT. Ourselves, our wives, and children, on our
       knees,
Are bound to pray for you both.
SIC. Live, and thrive!
BRU. Farewell, kind neighbours: we wish'd Coriolanus
Had loved you as we did.

CITIZENS. Now the gods keep you! 25
BOTH TRI. *Farewell, farewell. (Exeunt Citizens.)*
SIC. This is a happier and more comely time
Than when these fellows ran about the streets,
Crying confusion.
BRU. Caius Marcius was
A worthy officer i' the war, but insolent, 30
O'ercome with pride, ambitious past all thinking,
Self-loving,—
SIC. And affecting one sole throne,
Without assistance.
MEN. I think not so.
SIC. We should by this, to all our lamentation,
If he had gone forth consul, found it so. 35
BRU. The gods have well prevented it, and Rome
Sits safe and still without him.
(Enter an Ædile.)
ÆD. Worthy tribunes,
There is a slave, whom we have put in prison,
Reports, the Volsces with two several powers
Are enter'd in the Roman territories, 40
And with the deepest malice of the war
Destroy what lies before 'em.
MEN. 'Tis Aufidius,
Who, hearing of our Marcius' banishment,
Thrusts forth his horns again into the world;
Which were inshell'd when Marcius stood for Rome, 45
And durst not once peep out.
SIC. Come, what talk you
Of Marcius?
BRU. Go see this rumourer whipp'd. It cannot be
The Volsces dare break with us.
MEN. Cannot be!
We have record that very well it can, 50
And three examples of the like have been
Within my age. But reason with the fellow,
Before you punish him, where he heard this,
Lest you shall chance to whip your information

And beat the messenger who bids beware 55
Of what is to be dreaded.

Sic. Tell not me:
I know this cannot be.

Bru. Not possible.

(Enter a Messenger.)

Mess. The nobles in great earnestness are going
All to the senate-house: some news is come
That turns their countenances.

Sic. 'Tis this slave; 60
Go whip him 'fore the people's eyes: his raising;
Nothing but his report.

Mess. Yes, worthy sir,
The slave's report is seconded; and more,
More fearful, is deliver'd.

Sic. What more fearful?

Mess. It is spoke freely out of many mouths— 65
How probable I do not know—that Marcius,
Join'd with Aufidius, leads a power 'gainst Rome,
And vows revenge as spacious as between
The young'st and oldest thing.

Sic. This is most likely!

Bru. Raised only, that the weaker sort may wish 70
Good Marcius home again.

Sic. The very trick on't.

Men. This is unlikely:
He and Aufidius can no more atone
Than violentest contrariety.

(Enter a second Messenger.)

Sec. Mess. You are sent for to the senate: 75
A fearful army, led by Caius Marcius
Associated with Aufidius, rages
Upon our territories; and have already
O'erborne their way, consumed with fire, and took
What lay before them. 80

(Enter Cominius.)

Com. O, you have made good work!

MEN. What news? what news?

COM. You have holp to ravish your own daughters, and
To melt the city leads upon your pates;
To see your wives dishonour'd to your noses,—

MEN. What's the news? what's the news? 85

COM. Your temples burned in their cement, and
Your franchises, whereon you stood, confined
Into an auger's bore.

MEN. Pray now, your news?—
You have made fair work, I fear me.—Pray, your news?—
If Marcius should be join'd with Volscians,—

COM. If! 90
He is their god: he leads them like a thing
Made by some other deity than nature,
That shapes man better; and they follow him,
Against us brats, with no less confidence
Than boys pursuing summer butterflies, 95
Or butchers killing flies.

MEN. You have made good work,
You and your apron-men; you that stood so much
Upon the voice of occupation and
The breath of garlic-eaters!

COM. He'll shake your Rome about your ears.

MEN. As Hercules 100
Did shake down mellow fruit. You have made fair work!

BRU. But is this true, sir?

COM. Ay; and you'll look pale
Before you find it other. All the regions
Do smilingly revolt; and who resist
Are mock'd for valiant ignorance, 105
And perish constant fools. Who is't can blame him?
Your enemies and his find something in him.

MEN. We are all undone, unless
The noble man have mercy.

COM. Who shall ask it?
The tribunes cannot do't for shame; the people 110
Deserve such pity of him as the wolf
Does of the shepherds: for his best friends, if they

Should say 'Be good to Rome,' they charged him even
As those should do that had deserved his hate,
And therein show'd like enemies.
MEN. 'Tis true: $_{115}$
If he were putting to my house the brand
That should consume it, I have not the face
To say 'Beseech you, cease.' You have made fair hands,
You and your crafts! you have crafted fair!
COM. You have brought
A trembling upon Rome, such as was never $_{120}$
So incapable of help.
BOTH TRI. Say not, we brought it.
MEN. How! was it we? we loved him; but, like beasts
And cowardly nobles, gave way unto your clusters,
Who did hoot him out o' the city.
COM. But I fear
They'll roar him in again. Tullus Aufidius, $_{125}$
The second name of men, obeys his points
As if he were his officer: desperation
Is all the policy, strength and defence,
That Rome can make against them.
(Enter a troop of Citizens.)
MEN. Here come the clusters
And is Aufidius with him? You are they $_{130}$
That made the air unwholesome, when you cast
Your stinking greasy caps in hooting at
Coriolanus' exile. Now he's coming;
And not a hair upon a soldier's head
Which will not prove a whip: as many coxcombs $_{135}$
As you threw caps up will he tumble down,
And pay you for your voices. 'Tis no matter;
If he could burn us all into one coal,
We have deserved it.
CITIZENS. Faith, we hear fearful news.
FIRST CIT. For mine own part, $_{140}$
When I said, banish him, I said, 'twas pity.
SEC. CIT. And so did I.
THIRD CIT. And so did I; and, to say the truth, so did

very many of us: that we did, we did for the best; and
though we willingly consented to his banishment, yet it
was ₁₄₅
against our will.

COM. Ye're goodly things, you voices!

MEN. You have made
Good work, you and your cry! Shall 's to the Capitol?

COM. *O, ay, what else? (Exeunt Cominius and Menenius.)*

SIC. Go, masters, get you home; be not dismay'd: ₁₅₀
These are a side that would be glad to have
This true which they so seem to fear. Go home,
And show no sign of fear.

FIRST CIT. The gods be good to us! Come, masters,
let's home. I ever said we were i' the wrong when we ₁₅₅
banished him.

SEC. CIT. So did we all. But, come, let's home.
(Exeunt Citizens.)

BRU. I do not like this news.

SIC. Nor I.

BRU. Let's to the Capitol: would half my wealth ₁₆₀
Would buy this for a lie!

SIC. Pray, let us go. (*Exeunt.*)

SCENE VII. A CAMP, AT A SMALL DISTANCE FROM ROME.

(Enter AUFIDIUS *with his* Lieutenant.)

AUF. Do they still fly to the Roman?

LIEU. I do not know what witchcraft's in him, but
Your soldiers use him as the grace 'fore meat,
Their talk at table and their thanks at end;
And you are darken'd in this action, sir, ₅
Even by your own.

AUF. I cannot help it now,
Unless, by using means, I lame the foot
Of our design. He bears himself more proudlier,

Even to my person, than I thought he would
When first I did embrace him: yet his nature 10
In that's no changeling; and I must excuse
What cannot be amended.
LIEU. Yet I wish, sir—
I mean for your particular—you had not
Join'd in commission with him; but either
Had borne the action of yourself, or else 15
To him had left it solely.
AUF. I understand thee well; and be thou sure,
When he shall come to his account, he knows not
What I can urge against him. Although it seems,
And so he thinks, and is no less apparent 20
To the vulgar eye, that he bears all things fairly,
And shows good husbandry for the Volscian state,
Fights dragon-like, and does achieve as soon
As draw his sword, yet he hath left undone
That which shall break his neck or hazard mine, 25
Whene'er we come to our account.
LIEU. Sir, I beseech you, think you he'll carry Rome?
AUF. All places yield to him ere he sits down;
And the nobility of Rome are his:
The senators and patricians love him too: 30
The tribunes are no soldiers; and their people
Will be as rash in the repeal, as hasty
To expel him thence. I think he'll be to Rome
As is the osprey to the fish, who takes it
By sovereignty of nature. First he was 35
A noble servant to them; but he could not
Carry his honours even: whether 'twas pride,
Which out of daily fortune ever taints
The happy man; whether defect of judgement,
To fail in the disposing of those chances 40
Which he was lord of; or whether nature,
Not to be other than one thing, not moving
From the casque to the cushion, but commanding peace
Even with the same austerity and garb
As he controll'd the war; but one of these— 45

As he hath spices of them all, not all,
For I dare so far free him—made him fear'd,
So hated, and so banish'd: but he has a merit,
To choke it in the utterance. So our virtues
Lie in the interpretation of the time; 50
And power, unto itself most commendable,
Hath not a tomb so evident as a chair
To extol what it hath done.
One fire drives out one fire; one nail, one nail;
Rights by rights fouler, strengths by strengths do fail. 55
Come, let's away. When, Caius, Rome is thine,
Thou art poor'st of all; then shortly art thou mine. (*Exeunt.*)

ACT V

SCENE I. ROME. A PUBLIC PLACE

(ENTER MENENIUS, COMINIUS, SICINIUS *AND* BRUTUS, *THE TWO* TRIBUNES, *AND OTHERS.)*

MEN. No, I'll not go: you hear what he hath said
Which was sometime his general, who loved him
In a most dear particular. He call'd me father:
But what o' that? Go, you that banish'd him;
A mile before his tent fall down, and knee ₅
The way into his mercy: nay, if he coy'd
To hear Cominius speak, I'll keep at home.
COM. He would not seem to know me.
MEN. Do you hear?
COM. Yet one time he did call me by my name:
I urged our old acquaintance, and the drops ₁₀
That we have bled together. Coriolanus
He would not answer to: forbad all names;
He was a kind of nothing, titleless,
Till he had forged himself a name o' the fire
Of burning Rome.
MEN. Why, so: you have made good work! ₁₅

A pair of tribunes that have rack'd for Rome,
To make coals cheap: a noble memory!
COM. I minded him how royal 'twas to pardon
When it was less expected: he replied,
It was a bare petition of a state $_{20}$
To one whom they had punish'd.
MEN. Very well:
Could he say less?
COM. I offer'd to awaken his regard
For 's private friends: his answer to me was,
He could not stay to pick them in a pile $_{25}$
Of noisome musty chaff, he said 'twas folly,
For one poor grain or two, to leave unburnt,
And still to nose the offence.
MEN. For one poor grain or two!
I am one of those; his mother, wife, his child,
And this brave fellow too, we are the grains: $_{30}$
You are the musty chaff, and you are smelt
Above the moon: we must be burnt for you.
SIC. Nay, pray, be patient: if you refuse your aid
In this so never-needed help, yet do not
Upbraid's with our distress. But, sure, if you $_{35}$
Would be your country's pleader, your good tongue,
More than the instant army we can make,
Might stop our countryman.
MEN. No, I'll not meddle.
SIC. Pray you, go to him.
MEN. What should I do?
BRU. Only make trial what your love can do $_{40}$
For Rome, towards Marcius.
MEN. Well, and say that Marcius
Return me, as Cominius is return'd,
Unheard; what then?
But as a discontented friend, grief-shot
With his unkindness? say 't be so?
SIC. Yet your good will $_{45}$
Must have that thanks from Rome, after the measure
As you intended well.

MEN. I'll undertake 't:
I think he'll hear me. Yet, to bite his lip
And hum at good Cominius, much unhearts me.
He was not taken well; he had not dined: 50
The veins unfill'd, our blood is cold, and then
We pout upon the morning, are unapt
To give or to forgive; but when we have stuff'd
These pipes and these conveyances of our blood
With wine and feeding, we have suppler souls 55
Than in our priest-like fasts: therefore I'll watch him
Till he be dieted to my request,
And then I'll set upon him.
BRU. You know the very road into his kindness,
And cannot lose your way.
MEN. Good faith, I'll prove him, 60
Speed how it will. I shall ere long have knowledge
Of my success. (*Exit.*)
COM. He'll never hear him.
Sec. Not?
COM. I tell you, he does sit in gold, his eye
Red as 'twould burn Rome; and his injury
The gaoler to his pity. I kneel'd before him; 65
'Twas very faintly he said 'Rise;' dismiss'd me
Thus, with his speechless hand: what he would do,
He sent in writing after me; what he would not,
Bound with an oath to yield to his conditions:
So that all hope is vain, 70
Unless his noble mother, and his wife;
Who, as I hear, mean to solicit him
For mercy to his country. Therefore, let's hence,
And with our fair entreaties haste them on. (*Exeunt.*)

SCENE II. ENTRANCE OF THE VOLSCIAN CAMP BEFORE ROME. TWO SENTINELS ON GUARD.

(*Enter to them, MENENIUS.*)

FIRST SEN. Stay: whence are you?

SEC. SEN. Stand, and go back.

MEN. You guard like men; 'tis well: but, by your leave,
I am an officer of state, and come
To speak with Coriolanus.

FIRST SEN. From whence?

MEN. From Rome.

FIRST SEN. You may not pass, you must return: our
general 5
Will no more hear from thence.

SEC. SEN. You'll see your Rome embraced with fire, before
You'll speak with Coriolanus.

MEN. Good my friends,
If you have heard your general talk of Rome
And of his friends there, it is lots to blanks 10
My name hath touch'd your ears: it is Menenius.

FIRST SEN. Be it so; go back: the virtue of your name
Is not here passable.

MEN. I tell thee, fellow,
Thy general is my lover: I have been
The book of his good acts, whence men have read 15
His fame unparallel'd haply amplified;
For I have ever verified my friends,
Of whom he's chief, with all the size that verity
Would without lapsing suffer: nay, sometimes,
Like to a bowl upon a subtle ground, 20
I have tumbled past the throw, and in his praise
Have almost stamp'd the leasing: therefore, fellow,
I must have leave to pass.

FIRST SEN. Faith, sir, if you had told as many lies in
his behalf as you have uttered words in your own, you 25
should not pass here; no, though it were as virtuous to lie
as to live chastely. Therefore go back.

MEN. Prithee, fellow, remember my name is Menenius,
always factionary on the party of your general.

SEC. SEN. Howsoever you have been his liar, as you say 30
you have, I am one that, telling true under him, must say,
you cannot pass. Therefore go back.

MEN. Has he dined, canst thou tell? for I would not
speak with him till after dinner.

FIRST SEN. You are a Roman, are you? 35

MEN. I am, as thy general is.

FIRST SEN. Then you should hate Rome, as he does. Can
you, when you have pushed out your gates the very
 defender
of them, and, in a violent popular ignorance, given your
enemy your shield, think to front his revenges with the
 easy 40
groans of old women, the virginal palms of your daughters,
or with the palsied intercession of such a decayed dotant as
you seem to be? Can you think to blow out the intended
fire your city is ready to flame in, with such weak breath as
this? No, you are deceived; therefore, back to Rome, 45
and prepare for your execution: you are condemned; our
general has sworn you out of reprieve and pardon.

MEN. Sirrah, if thy captain knew I were here, he would
use me with estimation.

SEC. SEN. Come, my captain knows you not. 50

MEN. I mean, thy general.

FIRST SEN. My general cares not for you. Back, I say,
go; lest I let forth your half-pint of blood;—back,—that's
the utmost of your having:—back.

MEN. Nay, but, fellow, fellow,— 55

(ENTER CORIOLANUS AND AUFIDIUS.)

COR. What's the matter?

MEN. Now, you companion, I'll say an errand for you:
you shall know now that I am in estimation; you shall
 perceive
that a Jack guardant cannot office me from my son
Coriolanus: guess, but by my entertainment with him, if 60
thou standest not i' the state of hanging, or of some death
more long in spectatorship and crueller in suffering; behold
now presently, and swoon for what's to come upon thee.
The glorious gods sit in hourly synod about thy particular
prosperity, and love thee no worse than thy old father 65
Menenius does! O my son, my son! thou art preparing

fire for us; look thee, here's water to quench it. I was
hardly moved to come to thee; but being assured none
but myself could move thee, I have been blown out of
your gates with sighs; and conjure thee to pardon Rome 70
and thy petitionary countrymen. The good gods assuage
thy wrath, and turn the dregs of it upon this varlet here,
   —this,
who, like a block, hath denied my access to thee.

COR. Away!

MEN. How! away! 75

COR. Wife, mother, child, I know not. My affairs
Are servanted to others: though I owe
My revenge properly, my remission lies
In Volscian breasts. That we have been familiar,
Ingrate forgetfulness shall poison rather 80
Than pity note how much. Therefore be gone.
Mine ears against your suits are stronger than
Your gates against my force. Yet, for I loved thee,
Take this along; I writ it for thy sake,
And would have sent it. (*Gives him a letter.*) Another word,
   Menenius, 85
I will not hear thee speak. This man, Aufidius,
Was my beloved in Rome: yet thou behold'st.

AUF. You keep a constant temper.

(Exeunt Coriolanus and Aufidius.)

FIRST SEN. Now, sir, is your name Menenius?

SEC. SEN. 'Tis a spell, you see, of much power: you 90
know the way home again.

FIRST SEN. Do you hear how we are shent for keeping
your greatness back?

SEC. SEN. What cause, do you think, I have to swoon?

MEN. I neither care for the world nor your general: for 95
such things as you, I can scarce think there's any, ye're so
slight. He that hath a will to die by himself fears it not
from another: let your general do his worst. For you, be
that you are, long; and your misery increase with your
age! I say to you, as I was said to, Away! (*Exit.*) 100

FIRST SEN. A noble fellow, I warrant him.

Sec. Sen. The worthy fellow is our general: he's the
rock, the oak not to be wind-shaken. (*Exeunt.*)

SCENE III. THE TENT OF CORIOLANUS

(Enter Coriolanus, Aufidius, *and others.*)

Cor. We will before the walls of Rome to-morrow
Set down our host. My partner in this action,
You must report to the Volscian lords how plainly
I have borne this business.
Auf. Only their ends
You have respected; stopp'd your ears against 5
The general suit of Rome; never admitted
A private whisper, no, not with such friends
That thought them sure of you.
Cor. This last old man,
Whom with a crack'd heart I have sent to Rome,
Loved me above the measure of a father, 10
Nay, godded me indeed. Their latest refuge
Was to send him; for whose old love I have,
Though I show'd sourly to him, once more offer'd
The first conditions, which they did refuse
And cannot now accept; to grace him only 15
That thought he could do more, a very little
I have yielded to: fresh embassies and suits,
Nor from the state nor private friends, hereafter
Will I lend ear to. (*Shout within.*) Ha! what shout is this?
Shall I be tempted to infringe my vow 20
In the same time 'tis made? I will not.
(Enter, in mourning habits, Virgilia, Volumnia, *leading young*
Marcius, Valeria, *and Attendants.*)
My wife comes foremost; then the honour'd mould
Wherein this trunk was framed, and in her hand
The grandchild to her blood. But out, affection!
All bond and privilege of nature, break! 25
Let it be virtuous to be obstinate.

What is that curtsy worth? or those doves' eyes,
Which can make gods forsworn? I melt, and am not
Of stronger earth than others. My mother bows;
As if Olympus to a molehill should 30
In supplication nod: and my young boy
Hath an aspect of intercession, which
Great nature cries 'Deny not.' Let the Volsces
Plough Rome, and harrow Italy: I'll never
Be such a gosling to obey instinct; but stand, 35
As if a man were author of himself
And knew no other kin.
VIR. My lord and husband!
COR. These eyes are not the same I wore in Rome.
VIR. The sorrow that delivers us thus changed
Makes you think so.
COR. Like a dull actor now 40
I have forgot my part and I am out,
Even to a full disgrace. Best of my flesh,
Forgive my tyranny; but do not say,
For that 'Forgive our Romans.' O, a kiss
Long as my exile, sweet as my revenge! 45
Now, by the jealous queen of heaven, that kiss
I carried from thee, dear, and my true lip
Hath virgin'd it e'er since. You gods! I prate,
And the most noble mother of the world
Leave unsaluted: sink, my knee, i' the earth; *(Kneels.)* 50
Of thy deep duty more impression show
Than that of common sons.
VOL. O, stand up blest!
Whilst, with no softer cushion than the flint,
I kneel before thee, and unproperly
Show duty, as mistaken all this while 55
Between the child and parent. *(Kneels.)*
COR. What is this?
Your knees to me? to your corrected son?
Then let the pebbles on the hungry beach
Fillip the stars; then let the mutinous winds
Strike the proud cedars 'gainst the fiery sun, 60

Murdering impossibility, to make
What cannot be, slight work.
Vol. Thou art my warrior;
I holp to frame thee. Do you know this lady?
Cor. The noble sister of Publicola,
The moon of Rome; chaste as the icicle 65
That's curdied by the frost from purest snow
And hangs on Dian's temple: dear Valeria!
Vol. This is a poor epitome of yours,
Which by the interpretation of full time
May show like all yourself.
Cor. The god of soldiers, 70
With the consent of supreme Jove, inform
Thy thoughts with nobleness, that thou mayst prove
To shame unvulnerable, and stick i' the wars
Like a great sea-mark, standing every flaw
And saving those that eye thee!
Vol. Your knee, sirrah. 75
Cor. That's my brave boy!
Vol. Even he, your wife, this lady and myself
Are suitors to you.
Cor. I beseech you, peace:
Or, if you'ld ask, remember this before:
The thing I have forsworn to grant may never 80
Be held by you denials. Do not bid me
Dismiss my soldiers, or capitulate
Again with Rome's mechanics: tell me not
Wherein I seem unnatural: desire not
To allay my rages and revenges with 85
Your colder reasons.
Vol. O, no more, no more!
You have said you will not grant us any thing;
For we have nothing else to ask, but that
Which you deny already: yet we will ask;
That, if you fail in our request, the blame 90
May hang upon your hardness: therefore hear us.
Cor. Aufidius, and you Volsces, mark; for we'll
Hear nought from Rome in private. Your request?

VOL. Should we be silent and not speak, our raiment
And state of bodies would bewray what life 95
We have led since thy exile. Think with thyself
How more unfortunate than all living women
Are we come hither: since that thy sight, which should
Make our eyes flow with joy, hearts dance with comforts,
Constrains them weep and shake with fear and sorrow; 100
Making the mother, wife and child, to see
The son, the husband and the father, tearing
His country's bowels out. And to poor we
Thine enmity's most capital: thou barr'st us
Our prayers to the gods, which is a comfort 105
That all but we enjoy; for how can we,
Alas, how can we for our country pray,
Whereto we are bound, together with thy victory,
Whereto we are bound? alack, or we must lose
The country, our dear nurse, or else thy person, 110
Our comfort in the country. We must find
An evident calamity, though we had
Our wish, which side should win; for either thou
Must, as a foreign recreant, be led
With manacles thorough our streets, or else 115
Triumphantly tread on thy country's ruin
And bear the palm for having bravely shed
Thy wife and children's blood. For myself, son,
I purpose not to wait on fortune till
These wars determine: if I cannot persuade thee 120
Rather to show a noble grace to both parts
Than seek the end of one, thou shalt no sooner
March to assault thy country than to tread—
Trust to 't, thou shalt not—on thy mother's womb,
That brought thee to this world.
VIR. Ay, and mine, 125
That brought you forth this boy, to keep your name
Living to time.
Boy. A' shall not tread on me;
I'll run away till I am bigger, but then I'll fight.
COR. Not of a woman's tenderness to be,

Requires nor child nor woman's face to see. 130
I have sat too long. (*Rising.*)
Vol. Nay, go not from us thus.
If it were so that our request did tend
To save the Romans, thereby to destroy
The Volsces whom you serve, you might condemn us,
As poisonous of your honour: no; our suit 135
Is, that you reconcile them: while the Volsces
May say 'This mercy we have show'd,' the Romans,
'This we received;' and each in either side
Give the all-hail to thee and cry 'Be blest
For making up this peace!' Thou know'st, great son, 140
The end of war's uncertain, but this certain,
That if thou conquer Rome, the benefit
Which thou shalt thereby reap is such a name
Whose repetition will be dogg'd with curses;
Whose chronicle thus writ: 'The man was noble, 145
But with his last attempt he wiped it out,
Destroy'd his country, and his name remains
To the ensuing age abhorr'd.' Speak to me, son:
Thou hast affected the fine strains of honour,
To imitate the graces of the gods; 150
To tear with thunder the wide cheeks o' the air,
And yet to charge thy sulphur with a bolt
That should but rive an oak. Why dost not speak?
Think'st thou it honourable for a noble man
Still to remember wrongs? Daughter, speak you: 155
He cares not for your weeping. Speak thou, boy:
Perhaps thy childishness will move him more
Than can our reasons. There's no man in the world
More bound to 's mother, yet here he lets me prate
Like one i' the stocks. Thou hast never in thy life 160
Show'd thy dear mother any courtesy;
When she, poor hen, fond of no second brood,
Has cluck'd thee to the wars, and safely home,
Loaden with honour. Say my request's unjust,
And spurn me back: but if it be not so, 165
Thou art not honest, and the gods will plague thee,

That thou restrain'st from me the duty which
To a mother's part belongs. He turns away:
Down, ladies; let us shame him with our knees.
To his surname Coriolanus 'longs more pride 170
Than pity to our prayers. Down: an end;
This is the last: so we will home to Rome,
And die among our neighbours. Nay, behold's:
This boy, that cannot tell what he would have,
But kneels and holds up hands for fellowship, 175
Does reason our petition with more strength
Than thou hast to deny 't. Come, let us go:
This fellow had a Volscian to his mother;
His wife is in Corioli, and his child
Like him by chance. Yet give us our dispatch: 180
I am hush'd until our city be a-fire,
And then I'll speak a little.

COR. *(After holding her by the hand, silent) O Mother, mother!*
What have you done? Behold, the heavens do ope,
The gods look down, and this unnatural scene
They laugh at. O my mother, mother! O! 185
You have won a happy victory to Rome;
But, for your son, believe it, O, believe it,
Most dangerously you have with him prevail'd,
If not most mortal to him. But let it come.
Aufidius, though I cannot make true wars, 190
I'll frame convenient peace. Now, good Aufidius,
Were you in my stead, would you have heard
A mother less? or granted less, Aufidius?

AUF. I was moved withal.

COR. I dare be sworn you were:
And, sir, it is no little thing to make 195
Mine eyes to sweat compassion. But, good sir,
What peace you'll make, advise me: for my part,
I'll not to Rome, I'll back with you; and pray you,
Stand to me in this cause. O mother! wife!

AUF. *(Aside)* I am glad thou hast set thy mercy and thy honour 200
At difference in thee: out of that I'll work

Myself a former fortune. (The Ladies make signs to Coriolanus.)
COR. *(To Volumnia, Virgilia, &c.) Ay, by and by:*——
But we will drink together; and you shall bear
A better witness back than words, which we
On like conditions will have counter-seal'd. ₂₀₅
Come, enter with us. Ladies, you deserve
To have a temple built you: all the swords
In Italy, and her confederate arms,
Could not have made this peace. (*Exeunt.*)

SCENE IV. ROME. A PUBLIC PLACE

(ENTER MENENIUS AND SICINIUS.)

MEN. See you yond coign o' the Capitol, yond
cornerstone?
SIC. Why, what of that?
MEN. If it be possible for you to displace it with your
little finger, there is some hope the ladies of Rome, especially ₅
his mother, may prevail with him. But I say there
is no hope in 't: our throats are sentenced, and stay upon
execution.
SIC. Is't possible that so short a time can alter the
condition of a man? ₁₀
MEN. There is differency between a grub and a butterfly;
yet your butterfly was a grub. This Marcius is grown
from man to dragon: he has wings; he's more than a
creeping thing.
SIC. He loved his mother dearly. ₁₅
MEN. So did he me: and he no more remembers his
mother now than an eight-year-old horse. The tartness of
his face sours ripe grapes: when he walks, he moves like
an engine, and the ground shrinks before his treading: he
is able to pierce a corslet with his eye; talks like a knell, ₂₀
and his hum is a battery. He sits in his state, as a thing
made for Alexander. What he bids be done, is finished

with his bidding. He wants nothing of a god but eternity
and a heaven to throne in.

Sic. Yes, mercy, if you report him truly. 25

Men. I paint him in the character. Mark what mercy
his mother shall bring from him: there is no more mercy
in him than there is milk in a male tiger; that shall our
poor city find: and all this is long of you.

Sic. The gods be good unto us! 30

Men. No, in such a case the gods will not be good
unto us. When we banished him, we respected not them;
and, he returning to break our necks, they respect not us.

(Enter a Messenger.*)*

Mess. Sir, if you'ld save your life, fly to your house:
The plebeians have got your fellow-tribune, 35
And hale him up and down, all swearing, if
The Roman ladies bring not comfort home,
They'll give him death by inches.

(Enter another Messenger.)

Sic. What's the news?

Sec. Mess. Good news, good news; the ladies have
        prevail'd,
The Volscians are dislodged, and Marcius gone: 40
A merrier day did never yet greet Rome,
No, not the expulsion of the Tarquins.

Sic. Friend,
Art thou certain this is true? is it most certain?

Sec. Mess. As certain as I know the sun is fire:
Where have you lurk'd, that you make doubt of it? 45
Ne'er through an arch so hurried the blown tide,
As the recomforted through the gates. Why, hark you!

(Trumpets; hautboys; drums beat; all together.)

The trumpets, sackbuts, psalteries and fifes,
Tabors and cymbals and the shouting Romans,
Make the sun dance. Hark you! (*A shout within.*)

Men. This is good news: 50
I will go meet the ladies. This Volumnia
Is worth of consuls, senators, patricians,
A city full; of tribunes, such as you,

A sea and land full. You have pray'd well to-day:
This morning for ten thousand of your throats 55
I'ld not have given a doit. Hark, how they joy!
(Music still, with shouts.)
Sic. First, the gods bless you for your tidings; next,
Accept my thankfulness.
Sec. Mess. Sir, we have all
Great cause to give great thanks.
Sic. They are near the city?
Sec. Mess. Almost at point to enter.
Sic. We will meet them, 60
And help the joy. *(Exeunt.)*

SCENE V. THE SAME. A STREET NEAR THE GATE.

(Enter two Senators with Volumnia, Virgilia, Valeria, &c. passing over the stage, followed by Patricians and others.)

First Sen. Behold our patroness, the life of Rome!
Call all your tribes together, praise the gods,
And make triumphant fires; strew flowers before them:
Unshout the noise that banish'd Marcius,
Repeal him with the welcome of his mother; 5
Cry 'Welcome, ladies, welcome!'
All. Welcome, ladies,
Welcome! (A flourish with drums and trumpets. Exeunt.)

SCENE VI. ANTIUM. A PUBLIC PLACE

(Enter Tullus Aufidius, *with* Attendants.)

Auf. Go tell the lords o' the city I am here:
Deliver them this paper: having read it,
Bid them repair to the market-place, where I,
Even in theirs and in the commons' ears,
Will vouch the truth of it. Him I accuse 5
The city ports by this hath enter'd, and

Intends to appear before the people, hoping
To purge himself with words: dispatch. (*Exeunt Attendants.*)
(*Enter three or four Conspirators of* AUFIDIUS' *faction.*)
Most welcome!

FIRST CON. How is it with our general?

AUF. Even so ₁₀
As with a man by his own alms empoison'd,
And with his charity slain.

SEC. CON. Most noble sir,
If you do hold the same intent wherein
You wish'd us parties, we'll deliver you
Of your great danger.

AUF. Sir, I cannot tell: ₁₅
We must proceed as we do find the people.

THIRD CON. The people will remain uncertain whilst
'Twixt you there's difference; but the fall of either
Makes the survivor heir of all.

AUF. I know it,
And my pretext to strike at him admits ₂₀
A good construction. I raised him, and I pawn'd
Mine honour for his truth: who being so heighten'd,
He water'd his new plants with dews of flattery,
Seducing so my friends; and, to this end,
He bow'd his nature, never known before ₂₅
But to be rough, unswayable and free.

THIRD CON. Sir, his stoutness
When he did stand for consul, which he lost
By lack of stooping,—

AUF. That I would have spoke of:
Being banish'd for't, he came unto my hearth; ₃₀
Presented to my knife his throat: I took him,
Made him joint-servant with me, gave him way
In all his own desires, nay, let him choose
Out of my files, his projects to accomplish,
My best and freshest men, served his designments ₃₅
In mine own person, holp to reap the fame
Which he did end all his; and took some pride
To do myself this wrong: till at the last

I seem'd his follower, not partner, and
He waged me with his countenance, as if $_{40}$
I had been mercenary.
FIRST CON. So he did, my lord:
The army marvell'd at it, and in the last,
When he had carried Rome and that we look'd
For no less spoil than glory—
AUF. There was it:
For which my sinews shall be stretch'd upon him. $_{45}$
At a few drops of women's rheum, which are
As cheap as lies, he sold the blood and labour
Of our great action: therefore shall he die,
And I'll renew me in his fall. But hark!
(Drums and trumpets sound, with great shouts of the people.)
FIRST CON. Your native town you enter'd like a post, $_{50}$
And had no welcomes home; but he returns,
Splitting the air with noise.
SEC. CON. And patient fools,
Whose children he hath slain, their base throats tear
With giving him glory.
THIRD CON. Therefore, at your vantage,
Ere he express himself, or move the people $_{55}$
With what he would say, let him feel your sword,
Which we will second. When he lies along,
After your way his tale pronounced shall bury
His reasons with his body.
AUF. Say no more:
Here come the lords. $_{60}$
(Enter the Lords of the city.)
ALL THE LORDS. You are most welcome home.
AUF. I have not deserved it.
But, worthy lords, have you with heed perused
What I have written to you?
LORDS. We have.
FIRST LORD. And grieve to hear 't.
What faults he made before the last, I think
Might have found easy fines: but there to end $_{65}$
Where he was to begin, and give away

The benefit of our levies, answering us
With our own charge, making a treaty where
There was a yielding,—this admits no excuse.

Auf. He approaches: you shall hear him. 70

(Enter CORIOLANUS, marching with drum and colours; the commoners being with him.)

Cor. Hail, lords! I am return'd your soldier;
No more infected with my country's love
Than when I parted hence, but still subsisting
Under your great command. You are to know,
That prosperously I have attempted and 75
With bloody passage led your wars even to
The gates of Rome. Our spoils we have brought home
Do more than counterpoise a full third part
The charges of the action. We have made peace,
With no less honour to the Antiates 80
Than shame to the Romans: and we here deliver,
Subscribed by the consuls and patricians,
Together with the seal o' the senate, what
We have compounded on.

Auf. Read it not, noble lords;
But tell the traitor, in the highest degree 85
He hath abused your powers.

Cor. Traitor! how now!

Auf. Ay, traitor, Marcius!

Cor. Marcius!

Auf. Ay, Marcius, Caius Marcius: dost thou think
I'll grace thee with that robbery, thy stol'n name
Coriolanus, in Corioli? 90
You lords and heads o' the state, perfidiously
He has betray'd your business, and given up,
For certain drops of salt, your city Rome,
I say 'your city,' to his wife and mother;
Breaking his oath and resolution, like 95
A twist of rotten silk; never admitting
Counsel o' the war; but at his nurse's tears
He whined and roar'd away your victory;
That pages blush'd at him and men of heart

Look'd wondering each at other.
COR. Hear'st thou, Mars? 100
AUF. Name not the god, thou boy of tears!
COR. *Ha!*
AUF. No more.
COR. Measureless liar, thou hast made my heart
Too great for what contains it. 'Boy!' O slave!
Pardon me, lords, 'tis the first time that ever 105
I was forced to scold. Your judgements, my grave lords,
Must give this cur the lie: and his own notion—
Who wears my stripes impress'd upon him; that
Must bear my beating to his grave—shall join
To thrust the lie unto him. 110
FIRST LORD. Peace, both, and hear me speak.
COR. Cut me to pieces, Volsces; men and lads,
Stain all your edges on me. 'Boy!' false hound!
If you have writ your annals true, 'tis there,
That, like an eagle in a dove-cote, I 115
Flutter'd your Volscians in Corioli;
Alone I did it. 'Boy!'
AUF. Why, noble lords,
Will you be put in mind of his blind fortune,
Which was your shame, by this unholy braggart,
'Fore your own eyes and ears?
ALL CONSP. Let him die for't. 120
ALL THE PEOPLE. 'Tear him to pieces.' 'Do it presently.'
'He killed my son.' 'My daughter.' 'He killed my cousin
Marcus.' 'He killed my father.'
SEC. LORD. Peace, ho! no outrage: peace!
The man is noble, and his fame folds-in 125
This orb o' the earth. His last offences to us
Shall have judicious hearing. Stand, Aufidius,
And trouble not the peace.
COR. O that I had him,
With six Aufidiuses, or more, his tribe,
To use my lawful sword!
AUF. Insolent villain! 130
ALL CONSP. Kill, kill, kill, kill, kill him!

(The Conspirators draw, and kill Coriolanus: Aufidius stands on his body.)

LORDS. Hold, hold, hold, hold!

AUF. My noble masters, hear me speak.

FIRST LORD. *O Tullus,*—

SEC. LORD. Thou hast done a deed whereat valour will weep.

THIRD LORD. Tread not upon him. Masters all, be quiet;
Put up your swords. 135

AUF. My lords, when you shall know—as in this rage
Provoked by him, you cannot—the great danger
Which this man's life did owe you, you'll rejoice
That he is thus cut off. Please it your honours
To call me to your senate, I'll deliver 140
Myself your loyal servant, or endure
Your heaviest censure.

FIRST LORD. Bear from hence his body;
And mourn you for him: let him be regarded
As the most noble corse that ever herald
Did follow to his urn.

SEC. LORD. His own impatience 145
Takes from Aufidius a great part of blame.
Let's make the best of it.

AUF. My rage is gone,
And I am struck with sorrow. Take him up:
Help, three o' the chiefest soldiers; I'll be one.
Beat thou the drum, that it speak mournfully: 150
Trail your steel pikes. Though in this city he
Hath widow'd and unchilded many a one,
Which to this hour bewail the injury,
Yet he shall have a noble memory.

Assist. (Exeunt, bearing the body of Coriolanus. A dead march sounded.) 155